CASES IN BEHAVIOR MANAGEMENT

SECOND EDITION

SCOT DANFORTH
The Ohio State University

JOSEPH R. BOYLE
Virginia Commonwealth University

PEARSON

Merrill
Prentice Hall

Upper Saddle River, New Jersey
Columbus, Ohio

Library of Congress Cataloging-in-Publication Data

Danforth, Scot.
    Cases in behavior management / Scot Danforth, Joseph R . Boyle.—2nd ed.
        p.   cm.
    Includes bibliographical references.
    ISBN 0-13-171591-7 (pbk.)
    1. Classroom management.   2. Behavior modification.   I. Boyle, Joseph R.   II. Title.
LB3013.D34 2007
371.102′4—dc22   2006021053

Vice President and Executive Publisher: Jeffery W. Johnston
Executive Editor: Ann Castel Davis
Editorial Assistant: Penny Burleson
Production Editor: Sheryl Glicker Langner
Production Coordination: Thistle Hill Publishing Services, LLC
Design Coordinator: Diane C. Lorenzo
Cover Designer: Candace Rowley
Cover Image: Fotosearch
Production Manager: Laura Messerly
Director of Marketing: David Gesell
Marketing Manager: Autumn Purdy
Marketing Coordinator: Brian Mounts

This book was set in Garamond by Integra Software Services. It was printed and bound by R. R. Donnelley & Sons Company. The cover was printed by R. R. Donnelley & Sons Company.

Pearson Prentice Hall™ is a trademark of Pearson Education, Inc.
Pearson® is a registered trademark of Pearson plc
Prentice Hall® is a registered trademark of Pearson Education, Inc.
Merrill® is a registered trademark of Pearson Education, Inc.

Pearson Education Ltd.   Pearson Education Australia Pty. Limited
Pearson Education Singapore Pte. Ltd.   Pearson Education North Asia Ltd.
Pearson Education Canada, Ltd.   Pearson Educación de Mexico, S.A. de C.V.
Pearson Education—Japan   Pearson Education Malaysia Pte. Ltd.

10 9 8 7 6 5 4 3 2 1
ISBN: 0-13-171591-7

PREFACE

University students studying education and allied service fields often take courses in "behavior modification" or "behavior management." These courses are provided under the reasonable assumption that these professionals or professionals-to-be will need to know how to deal effectively with a wide range of behaviors that children and adolescents engage in. Specifically, teachers need to know how to develop and maintain a safe and peaceful atmosphere in which students can apply themselves to academic tasks and develop meaningful relationships.

Many of these university courses on "behavior management" suffer from a common weakness: a lack of thought-stirring opportunities for students to apply and discuss the behavior management theories and practices on the uncertain and multifaceted terrain of real social problems. The theories and techniques taught in the course tend to hang in the decontextualized air, leaving the students wondering what these ideas would mean if applied to actual child behavior problems that occur in schools. This book of cases directly addresses that need by providing realistic, context-rich narratives of behavior problems and social conflicts that developing professionals can ponder, puzzle over, discuss, and even disagree on.

Each case consists of two parts: a quick description of the problem incident itself and in-depth coverage of the salient background information concerning the individuals involved, the immediate social context, the school setting surrounding that immediate context, and aspects of the community at large. We have attempted to provide a broad range of behavior problem situations involving children and youth of all ages and abilities, ranging from preschool settings to high schools. We have distributed the cases across a variety of instructional settings, ranging from segregated special education programs to inclusive general education classrooms and traditional, noninclusive general education classrooms.

In our first edition of this book, we provided 38 cases of equal length. Based on reader feedback that we received, we have developed a second edition that includes 32 cases; 26 of the standard length we employed in the first edition, and six longer cases that provide much more depth and breadth of information.

These six expanded cases offer increased opportunities for teachers to fully utilize the various theoretical approaches, to investigate the problem occurrences in greater detail, substance, and complexity. Real-life behavior problems in the classroom are often like a moving target with multiple layers of information that just won't hold still. The more one explores, the more one finds both helpful and contradictory information. Clarity is accompanied by fuzziness and complications. The six expanded cases we have included in this second edition are intended to provide opportunities for advanced, deeper examination of behavior problem situations in all their complexity.

The structure of the text remains simple. There are two introductory chapters followed by the 32 cases. Chapter 1 gives a brief overview of social systems theory and the four basic theoretical models of human behavior and classroom management used by teachers. Social systems theory consists of a series of ecological rings extending from the child outward to the culture or society. It helps us to envision the many levels of social interactions, organizational structures, and cultural influences that play important roles in the creation and solution of child behavior problems. The four management theories we describe are the most commonly used by teachers: behavioral, psychodynamic, environmental, and constructivist. We introduce these briefly in chapter 1.

Chapter 2 articulates the general format for case analysis that may be applied to the cases. This format includes both immediate interventions and long-term intervention. Immediate intervention is the on-the-spot action taken to reduce a dangerous or threatening situation. Long-term activity involves careful planning and action designed to help a child or group improve behavior and interpersonal relationships. The chapter concludes with an example of case analysis by way of the general format and theories.

The 32 cases are arranged in random order. To help you access the kinds of cases you want to address, we have provided a case log (printed on the inside cover) that organizes the cases based on location (general classroom, special education classroom, outside school) and developmental level (preschool, elementary, middle, secondary).

ACKNOWLEDGMENTS

We would like to thank the following reviewers of the first edition for their valuable input and suggestions: Jim Burns, College of St. Rose (NY); Kathleen Gruenhagen, North Georgia College and State University; Darcy Miller, Washington State University; Philip Swicegood, Sam Houston State University; and Marshall Zumberg, Wayne State University (MI). We also thank Lisa Altemueller, Metropolitan State College of Denver; and Larry Beard, Jacksonville State University, for their review of this edition.

CONTENTS

Expanded cases in italics.

PART I
BASIC PRINCIPLES OF BEHAVIOR MANAGEMENT AND USING CASES

CHAPTER ONE

BASICS OF BEHAVIOR MANAGEMENT

Behavior management is an array of interventions created to help teachers influence the behavior of children and teach them to behave in positive and safe ways. These interventions are designed not merely to alleviate teacher anxieties of losing control but to help these professionals and the children they love create social atmospheres of cooperation, contexts in which children and adults can learn together, play together, and build quality relationships. Additionally, these interventions are useful for parents and community members who care for children. Often professionals are placed in consultative roles, helping and supporting parents and community members who may need assistance with child behavior problems.

In this chapter, we will provide a brief overview of four basic theoretical models of human behavior and classroom management. These models are not the final word on working with children and adolescents with behavior problems. They are the fundamental concepts and approaches that professional educators have devised over the years. The four basic models are:

1. Behavioral
2. Psychodynamic
3. Environmental
4. Constructivist

These four models differ in the way they define the sources or causes of human behavior. Also, they differ in the types of interventions they prescribe for teachers who are working with misbehaving children. Following each model summary, we will list five essential questions which an educator using that single model would use in analyzing a behavior problem situation.

Prior to presenting the four models of behavior and intervention, we will explain social systems theory (or ecological theory) as a broader, more general framework for viewing the complex lives and behavior of students. Social systems theory allows us to envision students not only as individuals with characteristics, abilities, and personalities. It assumes that no individual truly lives and stands alone. We are all social beings who are influenced and defined by our networks of relationships with other persons. Social systems theory helps us to take into account the many social webs in which an individual lives, grows, and learns. It should be viewed as a background map on which the interventions of the four models of behavior and intervention may be plotted and carried out. We will first present social systems theory and then outline each of the four models of behavior and intervention.

SOCIAL SYSTEMS THEORY

Social systems theory teaches us that we never deal with just a child or a child's behavior. We always deal with a child in context, a person embedded within and intimately connected to the surrounding physical and social world. Our efforts to aid or influence a child necessarily involve the contexts or ecologies in which that individual lives.

In social systems theory, child development is viewed as the continual adaptation or adjustment between an individual and the wide range of new and ever-changing social and physical environments. It is a progressive mutual accommodation that takes place throughout the life span between growing individuals and their life contexts. It is based on "the person's evolving conception of the ecological environment and his [or her] relationship to it, as well as the person's growing capacity to discover, sustain, or alter its properties" (Bronfenbrenner, 1979, p. 9).

Behavior is viewed as an expression of the dynamic relationship between the individual and the specific ecology in which the individual is situated or embedded (Plas, 1986; Rhodes, 1967, 1970; Swap, 1978). Behavior occurs in a setting that includes a specific time, place, object "props," human relationships, as well as previously established patterns of behavior (Scott, 1980). By "previously established patterns of behavior" we mean those ways of behaving that are habitual to an individual as he or she develops over time, and those past experiences that the individual brings to the setting in which the behavior is occurring.

Understanding the complexities of human behavior therefore requires more than the simple observation of an individual's behavior by one or two persons in a single setting, be that the school classroom or at home. It also requires an examination of the various systems of interaction of which an individual's behavior is only a part. In addition, to understand behavior one must take into account those aspects of the ecology or context *beyond* the immediate situation in which the individual is functioning that may affect the behavior (Bronfenbrenner, 1979).

What is an ecology or ecological system? We'll draw an analogy from natural science to explain this. Take the example of a single plant. If we were to attempt to explain why that plant is healthy and thriving or why that plant is weak and dying, we might merely analyze the plant itself. We could look closely at the leaves, the roots, the stalk, and so on. To think in ecological terms involves expanding that analysis to look at the way the plant interacts with the various aspects of the natural surroundings. We might then look at questions about the amount of precipitation, the amount of shade and sunlight, the chemical composition of the soil, and the influences of other plants and animals. The single plant and the surrounding ecology are enmeshed, inseparable. One cannot speak of the plant without also speaking of the surrounding system, the ecology in which that plant lives and plays a part.

Moving a step further, we realize that this local ecology is intimately tied to larger ecologies. A patch of terrain is merely one section of a larger forest. That single forest is part of a vast, complex, worldwide ecological scheme that includes global weather patterns and astronomical phenomena.

Expanding our plant metaphor to children, we can easily see that most children live within a number of local ecological systems. Typically, we look at the family system, the classroom/school system, and the peer friendship network as the most important local ecologies in a child's life.

Systems theorists tend to talk about the importance of congruence. Congruence is the "match" or "goodness of fit" between the individual and an ecology. Thurman and Marshall (1977) suggest that individuals whom persons judge to be "normal" are operating in an ecology that is congruent with that individual's actions. That individual's behavior is viewed as operating in harmony or in sync with the patterned norms of the social context. Thurman and Marshall (1977) further maintain that when there is a lack of congruence, the individual is viewed as either deviant (being out of harmony with the norms) or incompetent (lacking the necessary behaviors).

Congruence between the individual and the environment results in maximum competence and acceptance. According to Poplin and Stone (1992), an individual may be identified as having a disability when there is a mismatch between past and present experiences. The attitudes and behaviors that served the individual well in prior settings and situations are viewed as incongruent by persons within the new setting.

Bronfenbrenner suggests that the ecological contexts, or systems, in which an individual develops are nested, one inside the other, like a set of Russian dolls. He argues that the nested nature of the contexts is decisive in the individual's development as events take place within them. For example, he suggests that a child's ability to read may be related to the nature of the relationship between the child's home and school as well as the methods used in school to teach reading.

Any individual change must be viewed within the context of the larger social and cultural systems (Riegel, 1975). As previously stated, these ecological systems are nested and dynamic. These contextual levels were originally called the ontogenic self (Kurdek, 1981), the microsystem, the mesosystem, the exosystem, and the macrosystem (Bronfenbrenner, 1979). For our purposes, we will refer to these layered ecologies as the individual, interpersonal relationships, relationships between systems, group interactions, and society. We will now define and explain each of these five nested ecologies.

The Individual

Kurdek (1981) suggests that though Bronfenbrenner's ecological contexts provide an essential recognition of the complexity of human development, using only those contexts fails to take into account the individual differences or variations that each individual brings to his or her primary interpersonal relationship settings. He argues for the inclusion of the ontogenic system, suggested by Tinbergen (1951), within the social systems perspective. We refer to this system as "the individual."

The individual can be said to consist of an ever-changing array of personal characteristics. Among these characteristics are the cognitive, affective, communicative, social, and physical competencies that individuals bring to the settings in which they are living. Each individual has personal means for coping with the environment, including personality attributes, skills, abilities, and competencies.

Although social systems theory admits that the individual brings a set of personal characteristics to each social ecology, those characteristics are subject to the interpretation of persons who inhabit a given ecological system. For example, we may say that a personal characteristic of one child is her high degree of social skills. Yet that child's social skillfulness does not rest mysteriously somewhere inside her physical body or psychic structure. Her social abilities are interpreted by those persons who interact with and relate to her. This may even result in varied interpretations of her social skill development. Perhaps the child's fourth-grade teacher finds her to be cooperative and kind while her soccer coach describes her as unruly and disruptive. This difference may mean that the child does behave differently in these two social contexts. It also may reflect a difference in interpretation between the teacher and the coach. In this sense, we can see that while an individual brings a set of personal characteristics to each social setting, those characteristics are evaluated or interpreted by other persons who share the social setting.

Interpersonal Relationships

Human social systems are like spiders' webs. Each line of the web is a single relationship in the ever-changing social network. Over time, patterns of personal interaction and communication give each web, each social system, its own particular quality. In the home, a network of relationships occur, running like strings that connect all family members—parent and parent, parent and child, sibling and sibling. In the school, influential relationships occur between the child and teacher, as well as between the child and peers. Additionally, children (and adults, for that matter) often bundle themselves together into small groups, subsystems united by common interests and the bonds of friendship.

Relationships Between Systems

Relationships between systems may include the interrelations among home and school, home and service agency, home and neighborhood, and school and peer group. For example, students from minority cultural, ethnic, and linguistic groups may be challenged by the interrelationships between their home culture and the school culture and, as a consequence, be overrepresented as a group in special education. Parent-teacher collaboration and family–community service involvement

are included within this system. Relationships between settings include consideration of transitions, or the movement of the individual between educational and
employment settings.

Group Interaction

Group interactions describe the way that aspects of various systems relate to
each other. For example, changes in a parent's workplace may affect the family
system, producing new tensions or problems. This, in turn, may influence a child
so that he feels anxiety or fear. In this way, seemingly isolated ecologies interact
and affect each other. These interacting systems may include a parent's workplace, a sibling's classroom, and the various components of a school system.
Factors such as the availability of special education service programs, the goals
of educational programs in the community, and the selection of school
system–wide instructional materials and textbooks are examples of school-based
group interactions.

Society

At the broadest level of social systems theory, we understand that major institutions,
political activities, moral norms, and shifting philosophies occurring across society
intertwine to impact the life of an individual. A child who is raised in late twentieth-
century America experiences a social world vastly different from that of a child
raised in early eighteenth-century America or in late twentieth-century Guatemala.
The vast political, economic, and social world provides the context in which an
individual life is formed and understood.

    Daily, in a wide variety of settings and institutions, the persons and groups of
society are involved in the continuous making and remaking of cultural norms.
These norms are sometimes ambiguous. Sometimes there are clear guidelines for
human action and social interaction. The question "What is right?" is asked and
answered constantly as people go about their daily business. Often the cultural
norms that are enacted in public schools and other major institutions reflect the
values and belief systems of dominant groups. Simultaneously, though, alternative
norms are constructed by persons and groups that disagree with dominant and
socially mandated ways.

    In this societal mix of clarity, conflict, and uncertainty, most crucial to our
topic of behavior management is the moral question, "What is good or bad behavior?" Because no timeless, universal standards of child behavior have been etched
across the sky, determinations of what constitutes good and bad child behavior vary
greatly. Certainly, in the midst of this ambiguity, a variety of social forces influence
how parents and professionals view and evaluate the behavior of children.
Ultimately, ethical questions are decided by individuals and groups within actual
lived situations, the day-to-day sorting out of specific problems and possibilities.
We all make such decisions.

IMPLICATIONS OF SOCIAL SYSTEMS THEORY FOR BEHAVIOR MANAGEMENT

If there is one concept we would like readers to gather from social systems theory, it is this: An individual is inextricably intertwined by way of human relationships with social networks both small and large. If the general goals of behavior management practices are to help children both to improve their behavior and to take greater control over what they do, then social systems theory teaches us that there are many systemic points at which a concerned person may intervene to help a child or adolescent. We can envision a variety of possible interventions taking place at various points.

For example, imagine a 6-year-old boy named Philip. Ms. Sherman, his teacher, has struggled to help him improve his negative and disruptive behavior in his first-grade class. Philip tends to be easily frustrated and sometimes throws temper tantrums when he does not get what he wants. Without going into great detail, we can imagine many possible interventions occurring at various points. For the sake of this illustration, let's imagine Philip's first-grade teacher initiating five specific interventions, each focusing on a different ecological level. Each intervention could possibly influence Philip's feelings and behavior in positive and negative ways.

1. *Individual.* Ms. Sherman gradually teaches Philip what "anger" is, how it feels, how to notice when he is becoming angry, and how to manage his anger in less disruptive ways.
2. *Interpersonal relationships.* Ms. Sherman plans a number of times each week when she or her classroom aide and Philip can spend personal time together enjoying each other's company and improving their relationship.
3. *Relationships between systems.* Ms. Sherman talks extensively with Philip's mother about the problem, sharing ideas and concerns.
4. *Group interactions.* Ms. Sherman arranges for Philip and his mother to meet with the guidance counselor to discuss ways to help Philip learn to manage his anger.
5. *Society.* Ms. Sherman observes Philip closely to understand more fully when and why he actually becomes angered. She finds that he tends to want to keep objects like toys and school supplies to himself. He and many of Ms. Sherman's students do not like sharing with others. Ms. Sherman feels that much of American society engages in a competition to own goods and property as an attempt to be fulfilled. Ms. Sherman decides to attempt to teach her entire class to be more cooperative than competitive, more communal than selfish.

Although a nonprofessional might not address the situation with such a multidimensional approach, this example provides a glimpse of how interventions may be implemented at many ecological levels.

In the following sections, we describe the primary models of behavior management. Because these models have been developed primarily for use by professionals who deal directly with children in local ecologies, these models tend to emphasize interventions aimed toward the inner rings of the ecological circles. Note how each model has its own way of conceptualizing a behavior problem and intervening toward improvement.

BEHAVIORAL MODEL

Harkening back to the work of behavioral science pioneers like Watson (1930/1970), Thorndike (1932), Wolpe (1973), Bandura (1969), and Skinner (1974), the behavioral model is concerned with the scientific modification of observable behaviors. This is accomplished through the precise alteration of stimuli, the influential aspects of an individual's immediate environment. Behaviorists hold that environmental variables all but dictate an individual's behavior. From the standpoint of the behavioral model, all behavior is conditioned by external stimuli. Those behaviors that are conditioned and exhibited by a person are controlled by the environmental stimuli that immediately surround the individual.

The source of specific behaviors can be found in the environmental stimuli that reward, fail to reward, or punish. In this sense, the person's many behaviors are literally viewed as "responses" occurring in relation to specific stimuli in the environment. Interventions designed to change behavior involve the careful study of the stimuli that promote or discourage a given behavior. Once the specific stimuli are identified, then those stimuli may be altered in order to increase or decrease the probability that the targeted behavior will occur. In a nutshell, a behavior is changed through the strategic modification of the environmental stimuli that influence that behavior. This usually involves the introduction of reinforcers according to the behavioral principles of reinforcement.

There are five basic principles of reinforcement that should be followed in order to increase a target behavior (desired behavior to be increased). First, reinforcement or reward must be presented only when the target behavior is exhibited. Reinforcement is only effective if it is specifically applied to the target behavior. Second, the reinforcer should be presented immediately after the target behavior is exhibited. If a time delay between the target behavior and the reward occurs, the likelihood that the behavior will be increased is greatly reduced. Third, initially, the target behavior must be reinforced every time it is exhibited. Fourth, once the target behavior has been increased to the desired level, then reinforcement should occur on an intermittent basis. The behavior is maintained at the achieved level by a schedule of inconsistent reinforcement. Lastly, tangible reinforcers should be accompanied by social reinforcers such as kind words and supportive smiles.

The primary three applications of this model in behavior management are behavior modification (Alberto & Troutman, 1995; Schloss & Smith, 1998; Van Houten & Axelrod, 1993), functional analysis (Iwata, 1994; Reichle & Wacker, 1993; Repp, 1994; Sugai & Tindal, 1993; Umbreit, 1996), and Pre-Mod analysis (Kaplan, 1995).

Behavior modification assumes that behaviors are exhibited by an individual primarily as a direct function of the *reinforcers* that occur immediately prior (antecedent) and/or immediately after (consequence) the behavior. Altering antecedents and consequences of behavior thereby modifies the behavior. The procedure for implementing a behavior modification plan involves the following steps: (a) Select the specific behavior to be changed; (b) choose and introduce an influential reinforcer at the appropriate time; (c) design and consistently present the reinforcer according to the behavioral principles of reinforcement; and (d) monitor the behavior over time and evaluate the effectiveness of the intervention.

Functional analysis is a technique of behavioral intervention that adds the complexity of context to the task of understanding the environmental variables (antecedent and consequent events) that support behaviors. Sugai and Tindal (1993) describe functional analysis as "a temporally based direct observation procedure designed to examine the relationship between behavior and setting variables" (p. 86). They further state that the purpose of an observation is three-fold: (a) to collect a sample and a count of the behaviors exhibited by the individual, (b) to document behavior chains, series of behaviors in which the occurrence of one behavior seems to trigger or promote the exhibition of the next behavior, and (c) ultimately, to create an explanation for the individual's behavior that functionally links that behavior to events and behaviors occuring in temporal proximity (antecedents and consequences). Based on this functional explanation, variables may be strategically altered and behavior may be changed.

Pre-Mod analysis (Kaplan, 1995) adds emotional and cognitive dimensions to the strictly behavioral focus of functional analysis. Whereas functional analysis assumes that a specific observable is "caused" or "promoted" by environmental stimuli occurring immediately before or after the behavior, Pre-Mod analysis looks closely at the emotional state and general personality of the child as possible explanations for behavior. Maybe the child feels anxious or upset. Maybe the child is impatient or impulsive. Maybe the child simply is unable to do the desired behavior. Short-term emotional states like anger or sadness and long-term emotional conditions or temperaments such as depression or impulsivity are viewed as good explanations for child behavior. Simply put, the individual child's feelings, thoughts, and personality are seen as influential and important.

The general goal of Pre-Mod analysis is to figure out what prerequisite skills (attitudes, social skills, feelings, knowledge) a child needs in order to be prepared to learn the desired behavior. From there, a series of interventions can be designed to fully prepare the student to learn the positive behavior. The general Pre-Mod procedure involves four steps:

1. Name the desired behavior: What should the student be doing?
2. Name the specific attitudes, knowledge, emotions, and skills that are prerequisites for this child exhibiting this behavior. Perhaps the child does not understand the behavior or the situations in which the behavior fits. Perhaps the child is too angry to actually do this behavior. Perhaps the desired behavior is far beyond this student's social skill development.
3. Evaluate the child's ability to learn this behavior based on your list in step 2.
4. Based on the evaluation in step 3, design a series of interventions or lessons that will supply the child with the necessary prerequisite skills.

Five Essential Behavioral Questions

1. What is the *specific* behavior that is problematic?
2. Under what specific conditions does this behavior occur?
3. What are the antecedent and consequent conditions or events that tend to occur in conjunction with this behavior? (What happens before and after the behavior that might be supporting or reinforcing this?)
4. What is available that would be viewed as rewarding by the child or adolescent?
5. Who can systematically and consistently provide the rewards and how can this be arranged?

PSYCHODYNAMIC MODEL

While the behavioral model emphasizes the influential stimuli that exist physically *outside* a child, the psychodynamic model looks primarily *inside* the child. Based within a neo-Freudian understanding of individual psychology, this model views behavior as reflective of internal feelings and conflicts (Long & Morse, 1996; Redl & Wineman, 1951; Redl & Wineman, 1952). Wood and Long (1991) state this perspective clearly:

> When working with children and youth . . . adults need to acknowledge, accept, understand, believe, and appreciate that emotions are the powerful, personal engines that drive or generate human behavior. (p. 158)

Overwhelming feelings like anger, sadness, and confusion fuel overt behaviors. Often a child who is misbehaving is said to be "acting out" inner emotions, demonstrating how he or she feels at that moment. This demonstration is held to be, at least in part, unconscious or unintentional.

Psychodynamic interventions involve careful attention to the inner lives of children. Teachers employing the psychodynamic model believe in the daily priority of building trustful relationships with young persons in order to foster the development of self-esteem, personal insight, self-control, and social skills. Although this adult-child or teacher-student relationship comes to the forefront when a social conflict or stressful incident occurs, the teacher realizes that much of the relational groundwork for working with children experiencing emotional distress occurs during "down time," during the rather mundane moments when all seems calm and well. Buddying up to a student who is misbehaving is not the idea. Developing a form of intimacy and connection with students by talking, playing, and working together every day is the goal.

Additionally, the teacher utilizing a psychodynamic approach always remembers that he or she is not only dealing with overt behaviors. Observable behaviors, no matter how annoying or noxious, are the tip of the iceberg. Behaviors are pieces of surface evidence that teachers must interpret in order to understand the more pertinent emotions rumbling beneath. Working with a misbehaving child, in this model, involves more than attempting to influence how a child behaves. Lasting change is assumed to occur only from helping children to deal with the difficult feelings that stir beneath the behaviors.

The psychodynamic tradition advises teachers to help students to develop themselves in two specific ways: insight and trusting relationships. A student with a highly developed sense of *insight* has a strong awareness of her feelings and how those feelings are acted out in her behaviors. Additionally, the student is aware of when and why painful or troubling feelings tend to arise for her, the kinds of situations, interactions, and social dynamics that cause her own suffering. The practical side of insight occurs when students are able to isolate feelings from behaviors, realizing that while feelings of sadness and anger are very "normal" and acceptable, the translation of these feelings into behaviors is a matter of individual self-control. The student who becomes enraged and shouts obscenities at a peer can learn that the shouting behavior is not required by his feelings. Feeling the anger is probably unavoidable. What one does, the actions one takes, while angry can be far more socially responsible than shouting obscenities.

Insight is not easy to come by. It involves a rationality and reflective capacity that are often unavailable to a student feeling overwhelmed and driven by intense emotions. This is where *trustful relationships* come into play. When a student is caught up in the midst of powerful feelings, it often takes the support of caring adults to help that student feel a capacity and desire for self-control. The nonjudgmental support of a teacher can be especially crucial given the fact that most situations in which a student becomes engulfed in negative feelings occur within social conflicts. That is, children and adolescents often experience intense anger, sadness, guilt, and feelings of inadequacy during a conflict with other persons, during moments of strife and friction within relationships to people that matter to the student. The position of the teacher as a supportive, trusted adult can help to stabilize the emotional turmoil of difficult interpersonal conflicts and struggles, providing a sense of comfort and emotional safety, creating a soft place for a troubled student to land.

Behavior management strategies emerging from the psychodynamic tradition consist of counseling techniques and behavior influence techniques. We will briefly describe each.

Counseling techniques involve dialogues that build trust between troubled or misbehaving children and caring adults. The general goal of these dialogues or discussions is to provide emotional support to children experiencing emotional pain while promoting self-understanding, social awareness, problem-solving skills, and self-control. As with all forms of counseling, these methods require nonjudgmental listening and supportive forms of interaction on the part of the adult. Three useful examples of counseling techniques are: (a) active listening, (b) responding with understanding, and (c) Life Space Intervention (LSI).

George and Cristiani (1995) distinguish between the active listening necessary of a counselor in working with a troubled client and the typical forms of listening we use in social conversation. Within the give-and-take patterns of social conversation, we tend to listen while waiting to speak. The act of listening is somewhat shallow, occurring as one part of waiting to take the floor and speak. In contrast, *active listening* requires that a counselor or teacher set aside personal priorities and concerns to focus exclusively on the words, feelings, and perspective of the student who is speaking. This listening process occurs simultaneously on two levels. At the surface, the listener hears the words the student is expressing, the literal message. At a deeper level, the listener tunes in on the child's troubling predicament, the child's world at that moment, hearing and valuing that individual human experience. Although we all speak and listen every day, it is rare that someone is actually heard on this level and in this way. In psychodynamic theory, a teacher believes that such total listening is therapeutic for the student, providing a form of intimacy that supports the development of insight, moral concern, and healthy social relationships.

Responding with understanding, according to Egan (1975), takes active listening to the next step. Instead of evaluating the student's behavior or feelings, telling that student what is right or wrong about those actions and emotions, *responding with understanding* requires a teacher to reply to the student in a manner that demonstrates an understanding of the individual's predicament and perspective. This validates the student's worries, concerns, and perspective as real and worthwhile. Egan (1975) explains that when you respond with understanding, you:

- listen carefully to the other person's total communication—words, nonverbal messages, and voice-related cues;
- try to identify the feelings the person is expressing and the experiences and behaviors that give rise to these feelings;
- try to communicate to this person an understanding of what he or she seems to be feeling and the sources of these feelings;
- respond not by evaluating what he or she has to say but by showing your understanding of the other person's world from that person's point of view. (p. 137)

The goal of this form of listening and response is to help the student know and feel that he or she is understood. This supports and comforts the student, thereby greatly increasing the individual's ability in that moment to look closely and responsibly at the problem at hand. The individual is empowered by support and relationship.

Life Space Intervention (LSI) is a fairly complex counseling process that utilizes both active listening and responding with understanding. We'll briefly summarize this process here, but we recommend that interested readers consult Wood and Long (1991) for a more detailed explanation.

LSI is on-the-spot counseling that emphasizes both the feelings that underlie behavior and a direct, problem-solving approach to constructively addressing a current situation. Typically, an LSI occurs immediately after a problem event or behavior incident. The adult gently calms the upset child and then guides that child through a careful and honest reconstruction of the entire incident. The teacher asks questions that help the child to reconstruct an incident narrative, the precise sequence of events prior to and including the incident itself. This process brings the student into confrontation with the actual events, what others did and what he or she did. No blame is cast in this reconstruction. The initial goal is simply accuracy. Once the events have been set forth in full view of the teacher and student, then the teacher can encourage the student to locate the central issue of the matter, the primary conflict or misunderstanding that brought about the incident.

When both the teacher and the student can agree on the central issue or problem, then the teacher can support the student in accepting responsibility (not blame) for his portion of the problem. This approach assumes that all problems between persons are social and therefore responsibility typically is spread across participants. Sometimes the teacher may need to accept some responsible role in creating or perpetuating the problem.

With the problem identified and some degree of responsibility accepted, the student is prepared to work with the teacher to figure out how to solve or alleviate this situation. Perhaps some amends might be made, apologies offered. Perhaps there is a way to avoid such a problem in the future. Perhaps the student needs to develop specific social skills to do better next time. All these options are discussed in the problem-solving portion of the LSI. The LSI is completed with this practical discussion of what to do now, emphasizing the child's personal responsibility and self-control as an active problem-solver.

While most psychodynamic interventions attempt to address the feelings that stir beneath behaviors, Redl and Wineman (1952) have offered 12 *behavior influence techniques* that deal explicitly with "surface" behaviors. These surface management techniques were developed in recognition of the fact that classroom teachers simply do not have time to conduct counseling sessions for every minor behavior problem that pops up. The 12 techniques are:

1. *Planned ignoring.* Ignoring minor, annoying behaviors that children do to gain attention.
2. *Signal interference.* Nonverbal ways that adults communicate to children that behavior is acceptable or unacceptable (e.g., a sharp look, clearing the throat, thumbs-up, a nod and smile).
3. *Proximity control.* Standing closer to a misbehaving child in order to gently assert adult authority.
4. *Interest boosting.* Breaking the sometimes dull routine of school tasks either by reorganizing a student's work or by offering supportive and encouraging words that reinvigorate a child's desire to complete the tasks.
5. *Tension reduction through humor.* Be fun and funny to increase joy and decrease anxiety.
6. *Hurdle helping.* Providing needed academic and emotional support to a child who struggles in difficult tasks.
7. *Program restructuring.* Setting aside or recasting a specific activity that is not holding the student's interest and attention.
8. *Support from routine.* Using daily routines and rituals to create comfort and emotional security.
9. *Direct appeal.* Clearly stating what is going wrong and entreating a student's sense of fairness by asking for a change in behavior.

10. *Removal of seductive objects.* Withdrawing objects that sway the child's interest away from the task at hand.
11. *Antiseptic bouncing.* Removing an upset and disruptive student from the group or classroom in order to help the child calm down, gain control, and start fresh.
12. *Physical restraint.* In accordance with professional codes of ethics and local district policies, asserting safe physical control over a child whose behavior has become dangerous to self and/or others.

Five Essential Psychodynamic Questions

1. What difficult feelings is the child or adolescent experiencing (anger, sadness, frustration) when she or he misbehaves?
2. Why is the child or adolescent feeling this? (What is going on at the moment or in the child or adolescent's life that stirs these feelings?)
3. Is there a way to arrange for the child or adolescent to move away from the situation and cool down at the time these difficult feelings are rising up?
4. Is there a way to arrange for an adult that the child or adolescent views as caring and trustworthy to provide support and talk privately with the individual about these difficult feelings when these feelings occur?
5. Is there a way to increase the number and quality of trusting, caring relationships with adults in this individual's life?

ENVIRONMENTAL MODEL

The environmental model (e.g., Hobbes, 1966; Rhodes & Paul, 1978; Swap, 1978); focuses on the development of specific aspects of a child's immediate environments (home, school, neighborhood) that provide structure, support, vitality, and regularity. To some extent, what a person does (behavior) is inseparable from context. For example, imagine a child (or an adult!) waking up each morning in a different bed. The entire house has been rearranged. Also, the events of the day are completely unplanned. There is no continuity between one day and the next. The comfort of having some idea of what to expect is completely absent. Living within such an environmental context that offers no structure and no consistency would be emotionally difficult for most people. On the other hand, a few individuals would find such a lifestyle fascinating and enjoyable.

Of course, consistency can be overwhelming and stifling. Imagine a daily setting in which a regime of detailed routines is the master of all human activities. At 6:02 A.M., a 3-second bell sounds. There are 9 minutes to eat breakfast. The same menu of cornflakes, milk, and slice of dry, wheat toast is served every day. At 6:11, the breakfast dishes must be placed in the sink. The cereal bowl goes in first. This is followed by the toast plate, topped by the spoon, and so on. At this prisonlike extreme of order and regimentation, the living environment is humanly empty and even maddening.

The environmental model emphasizes the way the contexts in which a person lives greatly influences that person's behavior. There is no absolute formula for designing healthy contexts in which to live and learn. Individuals vary too greatly in demeanor and tastes for such certainty. Instead, the key is in fashioning contexts that match the personality and needs of the individual child. To this end, the environmental model focuses on the contributions of three specific areas of environmental organization to the behavior of children: time, physical space, and patterns of human interaction. We will briefly discuss each of these three areas of environmental management. Each area consists of a list of questions to help adults consider the way environmental details and arrangements foster desirable and undesirable behavior.

Time

The primary question to consider is: Are the activities of the day (week, month, year) organized in such a way as to promote emotional comfort, cooperative behavior, and personal fulfillment?

Additional questions that are helpful in analyzing time more carefully include:

Is the day scheduled too tightly (over-ordered) or too loosely (under-ordered) for this child?

Does the daily schedule include a balance of meaningful routines and opportunities for improvisation?

Is the schedule clear and understandable to the child?

What role does the child play in planning activities?

Are there specific aspects of the day in which behavior problems are more likely?

How can the daily activities be redesigned to avoid or alter these trouble spots?

Physical Space

The primary question to consider is: Are physical objects (such as chairs, tables, desks, lighting, and other materials) arranged in such a way as to promote bodily comfort, emotional ease, concentration to task, constructive communication, and positive relationships with others? Additional questions that are helpful in analyzing physical space more carefully include:

Does the physical space, including furniture, lighting, flooring, and materials, support the successful completion of the desired activities?

Is the room or area overcrowded? Too noisy? Unattractive?

Are the instructional or recreational materials adequate to support the tasks?

Do the children need help in organizing and using their own materials?

Do the children have adequate personal space for themselves and their belongings?

Patterns of Human Interaction

Patterns of human interaction within groups (families, classroom groups) are oft-repeated sequences of behaviors that often are maintained within habits and rules. Individuals and groups have habits, typical patterns of behavior that are repeated each day. To some extent, what an individual or group did yesterday is likely to be done today.

Rules often govern what happens. We should think of two different types of rules, explicit and implicit, each very powerful in explaining the behavior of individuals within group contexts. *Explicit rules* are the official rules, those that teachers post on the wall or schools write in schoolwide disciplinary policy handbooks. Explicit rules are often created and enforced by authority figures like parents and teachers to influence the behavior of children. *Implicit rules* are the informal or unofficial rules that govern and order interactions within the group. These are the cultural codes, practices, and manners that people tend to simply assume. For instance, the social practice of saying "excuse me" under specific types of situations is an implicit rule that is often (but not always) enacted. In the classroom, a variety of traditional student social practices would be considered implicit rules: addressing the teacher as Ms. or Mr.; asking permission before going to the restroom; storing personal materials in one's own desk or locker; using lower-volume voice tones in the library than in the gymnasium, and so on.

Additionally, we should realize that students themselves create and maintain a wide variety of implicit rules or social codes that influence and order their interactions and relationships. These micro-level behavioral codes involve various student roles (popular student, brainy student, class clown, etc.), friendship clusters, and the power relations among and between children. Social patterns concerning who interacts with whom, the style and content of those interactions, norms of communication and behavior, as well as activities of rejection, violation, and acceptance occur within the ever-flexing realm of implicit social rules. Even the way that explicit rules are handled (upheld, modified, transgressed) depends on the implicit rules of the classroom and school.

Patterns of behavior within a group can often be changed by altering the rules, explicit and implicit, that govern behavior. The primary question to consider in regard to patterns of human interaction is: How do the current habits and rules of the group promote or not promote the desired behaviors (cooperation, attention to task, and so on)? Additional questions that are helpful in analyzing patterns of human interaction more carefully include:

Are there clear procedures and norms for the many types of interaction? For answering questions? For talking to peers? For working together in small groups?

Are the rules of classroom behavior clear to all?

Are the rules conducive to respect and cooperation?

Are there unwritten rules that take precedence over the overt rules?

If so, do these unwritten rules support positive behavior and respectful interactions?

Are both written and unwritten rules respectful of the diversity of ethnic, cultural, and gendered norms of belief and behavior?

Is there sufficient opportunity for the children to seek meaningful changes in habits or norms that do not serve them?

Five Essential Environmental Questions

1. For each of the recent instances of misbehavior or conflict, describe the physical setting, time of day, activity, and participants. (Keeping observational field notes for a number of days can help with this.)
2. Do you notice any repeated patterns in regard to question 1?
3. Does the individual or group experiencing the behavior problems have any discomfort with the setting, time schedule, activity, or participants? (Ask!)
4. If you do notice patterns in how a certain setting, time of day, activity, or participants provokes or promotes the problematic behavior, what changes can reasonably be made?
5. What is your own (teacher's) role as a powerful element of the social context in contributing to or improving upon this problem situation? (This can be a tough one.)

CONSTRUCTIVIST MODEL

Derived from the works of scholars like Piaget (1954, 1970) and Bruner (1962, 1986, 1996), constructivism operates under the assumption that children are not passive receptacles of information but active constructors of personal and social meaning. Within their thoughts, feelings, words, and actions, children continuously create what is meaningful, valuable, and important to them. In this sense, children are constantly constructing personal knowledge about themselves and the world. This knowledge concerns personal identity, relationships with important others, cultural norms, and moral stances. From this perspective, we must keep in mind that even behavior we deem "inappropriate" is meaningful and important in some way to the child or children who do the behavior.

In addition to the personal meaningfulness of constructed knowledge, constructivism draws from the field of cultural anthropology in holding that much of what an individual "knows" and "believes" is shared with other persons (Bruner, 1996). In this sense, one's words and ideas are not merely individual inventions. They are shared cultural ways of understanding and thinking about human living. Persons of a common culture or subculture (like a classroom or school) tend to borrow ideas, beliefs, and words from each other. What is meaningful and important, those values concerning how a person should behave in specific types of situations, tend to be shared among groups of persons. Changes in those values and cultural codes occur on both the individual and the larger group level.

Additionally, drawing from the work of resistance theorists (Foley, 1990; MacLeod, 1995; McLaren, 1993; Willis, 1977), constructivists believe that cultural life is often filled with conflict and political strife. What counts as important and meaningful is not predetermined and fixed for all time. It is the subject of continuous struggle between various groups. Often these subcultural groups occur on the basis of social class, race, gender, sexual orientation, or other distinctions. Some dominant groups tend to set the values and other less dominant groups tend to resist or contest those values. This conflict occurs not only in the community but in the public schools. Drawing from the resistance theory knowledge base, constructivists realize that determining "the right behavior" or "the right thing to do" in a given situation is not a simple matter. Morally right behavior is an area of struggle within society and within schools between a variety of participants who disagree about basic values and ways of life.

Based on the theoretical stances stated above, the constructivist model emphasizes the development of individual moral autonomy (Fields & Tarlow, 1996), the building of supportive and diverse communities (Kohn, 1996), and the importance of caring for others (Henderson, 1996).

Moral Autonomy

Moral autonomy is an individual's ongoing sense of self as a responsible moral agent, a concerned evaluator of what is good and what is bad in each life situation. A child with well-developed moral autonomy is exploratory, continuously questioning herself about what is good. This questioning occurs not out of confusion but out of a pervasive feeling of concern for the well-being of self and others.

Fields and Tarlow (1996) present three general strategies designed to support the development of moral autonomy. These are for use when teachers deal directly with a student:

1. *Reciprocal respect.* Teachers often do not realize when they speak to children in harsh and cruel ways. We must remember that a child who is treated with respect will often reciprocate with respectful, cooperative behavior. Respect is something that teachers must earn. It is not something that can be demanded. Only fearful compliance can be demanded. Respect is earned by giving respect and by seeking similar dignified treatment in return.
2. *Related consequences.* If consequences (or punishments) are logically related to the misbehavior, then the student is more likely to learn a desirable lesson. The idea is that consequences should not simply inflict emotional suffering on the misbehaving child under the simplistic notion that bad behavior must be punished. Consequences should improve the problem situation itself and prepare a student for future moral decision making. For example, a child who steals can provide restitution of the stolen object. A child who makes a mess can clean it up. If a child physically or emotionally harms another person, the child can take action to reduce the victim's pain or discomfort. Obviously, this model of creating consequences for misbehavior does not involve preset, mandatory punishments. The use of related consequences requires flexibility so that the punishment can fit logically with the specific misbehavior.

Additionally, this approach often works best when consequences are actually negotiated between the student and teacher. This helps the student take responsibility for the misbehavior and the acts of restitution and resolution.

3. *Effective communication.* Here is where the constructivists appreciate and appropriate the counseling techniques of the psychodynamic model. Open communication free of judgments and shaming involves active listening and collaborative problem solving. Active listening means listening wholeheartedly without offering advice or direction. Collaborative problem solving means that solutions are not merely dictated by adults but are negotiated in good faith between child and adult.

Caring

After visiting many classrooms for student with severe emotional and behavioral difficulties, Morse (1994) finally realized the one characteristic shared by all gifted teachers. The students in these teachers' classrooms were fully convinced that their teacher was concerned about their well-being. Regardless of teaching techniques or tactics, the students knew completely that this teacher cared.

The act of caring for others is not viewed by the constructivist model as an individual behavior or a series of skills. A person who cares for others does not learn to do so single-handedly. Caring is always an aspect of relationship (Noddings, 1984, 1992). It is shared between two persons or among an intimately connected group such as a family or class of students. Caring is a quality of ethical, human connection in which each person is genuinely invested in the well-being of the other(s).

Central to this concept of an ethical, valuing relationship is a deep concern with the possibilities for the misuse of power within relationships between adults and children. A misuse of power violates what caring is all about. Henderson (1996) explains that teachers too often utilize "power over" students, a top-down form of authoritarian control that relies on the coercive influence of rewards, punishments, and threats. Coercion may produce short-term compliance, but it also creates children who are powerless and teacher-student relationships characterized by distance and lack of empathy. The concept of "power with" emphasizes the need for adult authority figures to share decision making with children. Children are invited into an ongoing and open dialogue with adults to make decisions concerning what is best for all members of the class or group. Such involvement in the building of an interdependent community allows children to feel responsible for themselves and their community.

Community-Building

Both Henderson (1996) and Kohn (1996) emphasize the need for schools to build democratic communities of social cohesion that value the many forms of human diversity. Henderson (1996) presents a complete community-building protocol for classroom teachers to build a supportive unit among their students. Although this protocol is too long to summarize here, we can point out some highlights of the approach. Community cannot be mandated by way of rules. It can be fostered gradually by a teacher who feels comfortable sharing power and responsibility.

The teacher who builds community reflects repeatedly on both the distribution of power and the quality of interactions within the social group. The goal is to lead a group of students to become caring equals, collaborators personally involved in co-constructing a learning community. Henderson emphasizes that teachers can be strategic and purposeful actors in encouraging the development of such a democratic community in which students feel both personally empowered and socially interdependent. The central component of this growing unity is the "classroom covenant" (p. 139), a solemn agreement that is gradually discussed and negotiated by all participants. This covenant is a binding document that describes the duties, rights, and obligations of each member of the class. It serves as a moral, communal guide for future activities and interactions. This covenant is a living document, open to possible renegotiation as community needs and problems change.

Five Essential Constructivist Questions

1. Describe the qualities of (dis)connectedness, (dis)unity, and (un)caring within the community or group where the behavior problems occur. (Community or group could mean classroom, Boy Scout troop, family, or any small network of relationships.)
2. How do you think the lack of (dis)connectedness, (dis)unity, and (un)caring within the community or group has encouraged or precipitated this behavior problem?
3. Does the individual (or individuals) in question feel respected and loved within the community or group? If not, why not?
4. How is power distributed (equally? unequally?) and used (respectfully? disrespectfully?) within the community or group? How could power distribution and use influence behavior?
5. How can the sense of connectedness, unity, and caring be improved in such a way as to provide better support for the person or persons experiencing behavior problems?

 SUMMARY

In this chapter, we have provided a brief overview of behavior management. This has included a description of social systems theory and overviews of four models of behavior management. We have presented the various social systems as interpersonal networks in which an individual is embedded. Interventions directed to help an individual feel or behave better may occur at various points in these systems. Our purpose in providing an overview of models of behavior management has been to allow readers the greatest flexibility of strategy and style in working with a problem of childhood misbehavior. The models differ greatly in how they view children, behavior problems, and the role of the teacher in relation to the child or children. We encourage our readers to consider each model carefully in designing and implementing interventions.

In the second chapter, we will explain a specific process for analyzing the many behavior problem cases presented in the remainder of the book. This analytic process should serve as one useful way of approaching the cases, for understanding the situation and creating possible interventions that would be effective or helpful.

REFERENCES

Alberto, P. A., & Troutman, A. C. (1995). *Applied behavior analysis for teachers: Influencing student performance.* Upper Saddle River, NJ: Merrill/Prentice Hall.

Bandura, A. (1969). *Principles of behavior modification.* New York: Holt, Rinehart and Winston.

Bronfenbrenner, U. (1979). *The ecology of human development.* Cambridge, MA: Harvard University Press.

Bruner, J. S. (1962). *On knowing: Essays for the left hand.* Cambridge, MA: Belknap Press of Harvard University Press.

Bruner, J. S. (1986). *Actual minds, possible worlds.* Cambridge, MA: Harvard University Press.

Bruner, J. (1996). *The culture of education.* Cambridge, MA: Harvard University Press.

Egan, G. (1975). *You & me: The skills of communicating and relating to others.* Monterey, CA: Brooks/Cole.

Fields, M. V., & Tarlow, M. C. (1996). Constructivist approaches to classroom management for students with disabilities. In W. Stainback & S. Stainback (Eds.), *Controversial issues confronting special education* (pp. 169–183). Boston: Allyn & Bacon.

Foley, D. E. (1990). *Learning capitalist culture.* Philadelphia: University of Pennsylvania Press.

George, R. L., & Cristiani, T. S. (1995). *Counseling: Theory and practice.* Boston: Allyn & Bacon.

Henderson, J. G. (1996). *Reflective teaching.* New York: Macmillan.

Hobbes, N. (1966). Helping disturbed children: Psychological and educational strategies. *American Psychologist, 21*(12), 1105–1115.

Iwata, B. A. (1994). Functional analysis methodology: Some closing comments. *Journal of Applied Behavior Analysis, 27*(2), 413–18.

Kaplan, J. S. (1995). *Beyond behavior modification: A cognitive-behavioral approach to behavior management in the school.* Austin, TX: PRO-ED.

Kohn, A. (1996). *Beyond discipline: From compliance to community.* Alexandria, VA: Association for Supervision and Curriculum Development.

Kurdek, L. A. (1981). An integrative perspective on children's divorce adjustment. *American Psychology, 36*(8), 856–77.

Long, N. J., & Morse, W. C. (1996). *Conflict in the classroom.* Austin, TX: PRO-ED.

MacLeod, J. (1995). *Ain't no makin' it.* Boulder, CO: Westview Press.

McLaren, P. (1993). *Schooling as a ritual performance.* New York: Routledge.

Morse, W. C. (1994). The role of caring in teaching children with behavior problems. *Contemporary Education, 65,* 3.

Noddings, N. (1984). *Caring, a feminine approach to ethics and moral education.* Berkeley: University of California Press.

Noddings, N. (1992). *The challenge to care in schools: An alternative approach to education*. New York: Teachers College Press.

Piaget, J. (1954). *The construction of reality in the child*. New York: Basic Books.

Piaget, J. (1970). *The child's conception of physical causality*. London: Routledge & Kegan Paul.

Plas, J. M. (1986). *Systems psychology in the schools*. Elmsford, NY: Pergamon Books.

Poplin, M. S., & Stone, S. (1992). Paradigm shifts in instructional strategies. In W. Stainback & S. Stainback (Eds.), *Controversial issues confronting special education*. Boston: Allyn & Bacon.

Redl, F., & Wineman D. (1951). *Children who hate: The disorganization and breakdown of behavior controls*. New York: Free Press.

Redl, F., & Wineman, D. (1952). *Controls from within: Techniques for the treatment of the aggressive child*. Glencoe, IL: Free Press.

Reichle, J., & Wacker, D. (1993). *Communicative alternatives to challenging behavior: Integrating functional assessment and interventional strategies*. Baltimore: Brookes.

Reigel, K. F. (1975). Toward a dialectical theory of development. *Human Development, 18*, 50–64.

Repp, A. (1994). Comments on functional analysis procedures for school-based behavior problems. *Journal of Applied Behavior Analysis, 27*(2), 409–11.

Rhodes, W. C. (1967). The disturbing child: A problem of ecological management. *Exceptional Children, 33*, 449–455.

Rhodes, W. C. (1970). A community participation analysis of emotional disturbance. *Exceptional Children, 36*, 309–314.

Rhodes, W. C., & Paul, J. L. (1978). *Emotionally disturbed and deviant children: New views and approaches*. Upper Saddle River, NJ: Prentice Hall.

Schloss, P. J., & Smith, M. A. (1998). *Applied behavior analysis in the classroom*. Boston: Allyn & Bacon.

Scott, M. (1980). Ecological theory and methods of research in special education. *Journal of Special Education, 4*, 279–294.

Skinner, B. F. (1974). *About behaviorism*. New York: Knopf.

Sugai, G. M., & Tindal, G. A. (1993). *Effective school consultation: An interactive approach*. Pacific Grove, CA: Brooks/Cole.

Swap, S. M. (1978). The ecological model of emotional disturbance in children: A status report and proposed synthesis. *Behavioral Disorders, 3*(3) 186–196.

Thorndike, E. L. (1932). *The fundamentals of learning*. New York: Teachers College Press.

Thurman, E. D., & Marshall, M. J. (1977). Clinical evaluation and coordination of services: An ecological model. *Exceptional Children, 44*, 16–22.

Tinbergen, N. (1951). *The study of instinct*. London: Oxford University Press.

Umbreit, J. (1996). Functional analysis of disruptive behavior in an inclusive classroom. *Journal of Early Intervention, 20*(1), 18–29.

Van Houten, R., & Axelrod, S. (1993). *Behavior analysis and treatment*. New York: Plenum Press.

Watson, J. B. (1930/1970). *Behaviorism*. New York: W. W. Norton.

Willis, P. (1977). *Learning to labour*. Farnborough, England: Saxon House.

Wolpe, J. (1973). *The practice of behavior therapy*. New York: Pergamon Press.

Wood, M. M., & Long, N. J. (1991). *Life space intervention*. Austin, TX: PRO-ED.

CHAPTER **TWO**

HOW TO ANALYZE A CASE

In this chapter we present a format for case analysis that may be applied to the cases throughout the remainder of the book. This format will include both immediate intervention and long-term intervention. Immediate intervention is on-the-spot action taken to reduce a dangerous or threatening situation. Long-term intervention involves careful planning and action designed to help a child or group improve behavior and relationships. Both types of intervention are salient for classroom teachers concerned with behavior problems at school and for professionals who consult with parents and community members who care for children in non-school settings.

After presenting the case analysis format, we will apply it to a behavior problem case. Our purpose is to provide a concrete example of how a case may be analyzed to produce a number of possible effective interventions.

CRITICAL REFLECTION AS THOUGHTFUL CASE ANALYSIS

Cases attempt to imitate the complexities of real life by refusing to submit to simplistic treatments. Although one can respond to complicated, multidimensional cases or real-life situations with quick, knee-jerk judgments, we believe that good teaching and effective behavior management require a more thoughtful process called *critical reflection*. This means thinking beyond one's immediate, armchair appraisal of a situation to consider alternative explanations that recast the scenario in very different lights. The teacher or professional who demonstrates critical reflection is able to view a situation from various perspectives and through a number of different theoretical lenses. Critical reflection combines mental flexibility with moral concern for the well-being of all persons involved.

Harrington, Quinn-Leering, and Hodson (1996) borrow heavily from the work of philosopher John Dewey in defining critical reflection according to three distinct elements: open-mindedness, responsibility, and wholeheartedness. Each of these calls upon an educator to analyze situations in a way that generally goes beyond egocentrism, moving out from the confined logic of one's own standpoint to broader dimensions and alternative ways of understanding. The impetus to move beyond one's own logic, beyond the comfort of one's usual way of seeing things, arises from the assumption that one's own perspective is inevitably limited and faulty. Continuous expansion of this perspective and reconsideration of personal beliefs about one's students will enable a teacher to broaden his or her array of useful techniques and skills.

Open-mindedness is the ability and willingness to recognize and value the validity of other perspectives beyond one's own, to realize that one's own way of viewing or describing a situation is not necessarily the best. This is a matter of remaining fallible and flexible, of attempting to be helpful instead of trying to be right. Seeing beyond the scope of one's usual way of viewing students and behavior problems is a difficult matter. We all tend not to notice our own blind spots, to remain unaware of what we are missing, as we move through the day within the limitations of our personal ideologies and understandings. Cultivating open-mindedness often involves developing vulnerability to new and even "strange" ideas.

Responsibility is the ability and willingness to examine the possible ethical and political consequences of one's choices, to realize that whatever one chooses to do will affect the lives of others in both foreseen and unforeseen ways. This is a matter of fully owning the many positive and negative ways in which one's actions might influence the lives of others, regardless of how things turn out. Blaming a student for not responding to a teacher's intervention is the direct opposite of responsibility. Students have no obligation to behave as we predict they will. Accepting one's limitations and fallibility as a professional demonstrates responsibility.

Wholeheartedness is the ability and willingness to identify the limitations of one's own reasoning and assumptions when making a decision, to understand the partial nature of any description of a situation, to appreciate the biases and values that inhabit one's own way of defining a problem and offering solutions. This is a matter of knowing yourself, your unique perspective, and where you are coming from as you look at human problem situations. A teacher can develop this kind of self-knowledge through examination of his or her personal biography, analyzing how the current way of viewing students and teaching is the culmination of years of personal experience (Danforth, 1997).

Ideally, these three aspects of critical reflection will be evident in the way one defines problems, designs immediate and long-term interventions, and evaluates the results of interventions.

For university instructors using this book as part of a course in classroom or behavior management, we provide an evaluation rubric (Table 2.1) that incorporates critical reflection and other pertinent performance criteria. This rubric is designed for the evaluation of an individual student's written case analysis. It also could be easily used for the evaluation of oral analyses of cases.

IMMEDIATE INTERVENTION

A toy flies across the room. A hand reaches out and grabs a clump of hair. Shouts and anger and threats ring out. A fist flies and blood is drawn. It can all happen so fast.

TABLE 2.1   Evaluation Rubric for Students' Written Analyses of Cases

Evaluation Component	Good	Acceptable	Poor
Problem Identification	Clearly and fully describes problems in (a) multiple useful ways or (b) the most useful way, while remaining true to the facts of the case	Adequately describes problems in (a) multiple useful ways or (b) the most useful way, while remaining true to the facts of the case	Fails to describe problems in (a) multiple useful ways or (b) the most useful way, while remaining true to the facts of the case
Critical Reflection*	Fully demonstrates open-mindedness, responsibility, and wholeheartedness*	Demonstrates an adequate degree of open-mindedness, responsibility, and wholeheartedness*	Fails to demonstrate open-mindedness, responsibility, and wholeheartedness*
Use of Theoretical Concepts and Vocabulary	Fully utilizes the theory(ies) of behavior management that are suitable and useful for the particular case	Adequately utilizes the theory(ies) of behavior management that are suitable and useful for the particular case	Fails to utilize the theory(ies) of behavior management that are suitable and useful for the particular case
Plan of Action	Clearly and fully describes useful, logically reasonable short- and long-term interventions as necessitated by the case	Adequately describes useful, logically reasonable short- and long-term interventions as necessitated by the case	Fails to describe useful, logically reasonable short- and long-term interventions as necessitated by the case
Evaluation of Plan of Action	Provides ample evidence that most drawbacks or limitations of short- and long-term interventions have been considered	Provides some evidence that most drawbacks or limitations of short- and long-term interventions have been considered	Provides no evidence that most drawbacks or limitations of short- and long-term interventions have been considered
Organization, Presentation, and Grammar	Writing is well organized, logically presented, and grammatically correct	Writing is adequate in regard to organization, logical presentation, and grammatical correctness	Writing is inadequate in regard to organization, logical presentation, and grammatical correctness

Source: From an unpublished evaluative rubric graciously supplied by Rita Silverman of Pace University.

*From "Written Case Analyses and Critical Reflection," by H. L. Harrington, K. Quinn-Leering, & L. Hodson, 1996, *Teaching and Teacher Education, 12*(1), 25–37.

Often teachers must react quickly to problem situations. A conflict between children or an individual's behavior has escalated to levels that threaten safety and demand immediate action. Such intervention does not involve systems of observation and careful planning. There is no time to sit down with a colleague or a friend and design a plan of action.

What caring adults can do is be prepared in advance. Preparation primarily involves anticipation, having a clear mental picture of what you can do if a problem arises. This section provides an outline of priorities and immediate actions that professionals can take to defuse a dangerous or threatening situation.

There are three basic goals of immediate intervention. We list them in order of priority:

1. Ensure physical safety.
2. Attend to the emotional well-being of those most centrally involved.
3. Return the setting to a state of order and peace.

Ensuring Physical Safety

The physical safety of both the misbehaving child(ren) and others is the greatest priority. Intervention for this purpose may involve the use of physical means, language (talking to the threatening child and others), and removal of children from the area. The goal is to quickly and safely eliminate the possibility of violence and harm to any person. This requires a cool head, an even voice tone, and decisive action. Remember, it is possible that an intervention will actually further exacerbate the problem, increasing the danger to all.

For example, a 7-year-old boy holding a pair of scissors over his head chases a peer. Defusing the danger of the situation requires that the child either give up the scissors or at least stop brandishing them as a weapon. Simple words of direction may do the trick. Yet simply telling an angry child to hand over the scissors may have no impact. Physically grasping the boy's arm and pulling the scissors from his hand may be necessary. Also, adults may need to move the boy to another room or area. A word of warning: Professionals who engage in any interventions utilizing physical force should consult codes of professional ethics and school district or agency guidelines concerning such activity. Physically subduing acting-out children should not be taken lightly.

Obviously, there are many risks to the adult and child in situations like this. Additionally, we must realize that dealing with a 7-year-old waving a pair of scissors and a 15-year-old armed with a knife are not the same thing. A professional must be aware of her or his own physical ability. Some adults can easily catch a running 7-year-old and snatch the scissors. Some adults may not be able to do this athletic feat.

We must always remember that standing up physically to an angry, possibly violent child or adolescent is a serious undertaking. An adult attempting to physically subdue a violent child should proceed with great caution in order to avoid injuring not only him- or herself but the child and others in the vicinity. When in doubt (and doubt is well advised in a dangerous situation), clear the room or area of peers and adults. This action removes possible targets of violent action. Often it is better to remove possible victims rather than directly taking on the threatening individual. Additionally, for professionals who deal with violent and threatening situations regularly, we recommend a complete training course in crisis intervention.

Attending to Emotional Well-Being

Once the danger has been successfully eliminated, emotions continue to run full and fast. Hearts are pounding, hands are sweating. All involved, including the misbehaving child or children, need to deal with the intense feelings that accompany such an incident. If feelings are ignored, other problems and conflicts are likely to follow.

Wood and Long (1991) describe this process as providing emotional first aid. In a sense, the emotions of all involved have been laid bare, opened like a wound. Immediate attention is required in order to support and vent intense feelings and confirm that a state of safety and peace has been restored. Simply put, this process involves talking to children about their feelings in a supportive manner. Adults need to listen and value the words of children and assure them their feelings are real and normal. Finally, adults must provide reassurance that all is well. As Wood and Long (1991, p. 162) say, the general message is, "It's okay to feel like this; it will get better."

Returning to Order and Peace

Of course, intervening to eliminate physical danger and addressing the intense emotions of all involved means little if the situation is not quickly guided back to a comfortable state of order and peace. Once emotions have been discussed and persons feel able to return to their typical activities, it is important to return to business as usual. We do not wish to encourage any form of denial in which everyone pretends that things are okay when no one actually feels safe and comfortable. The order and peace of our usual habits cannot be forced or artificially contrived. Additionally, be aware that not all individuals restore themselves to calm and return to their usual business at the same speed. In a school classroom, some students may feel ready to return to their academic work within minutes after a serious upheaval. Others, particularly those most involved in the incident, may take substantially more time to feel calm and able to reengage in the activities of the day.

Long-Term Intervention

If a single incident of misbehavior occurred, strategies of behavior management would hardly be necessary. Behavior management interventions are designed to create and maintain change in ongoing patterns of negative behavior. We call these *long-term interventions* because, unlike immediate interventions, they are designed and implemented for the purposes of promoting lasting, positive change in patterns of individual and/or group behavior.

Exactly what does and does not constitute a behavior problem requiring long-term intervention can be the subject of much debate. Behavior that one person finds intolerable and even immoral is deemed by another to be completely acceptable. We encourage professionals and parents to discuss these matters with trusted and knowledgeable colleagues and friends. There are no absolutes when deciding whether to intervene or allow behavior to continue. To some extent, we can understand that time and nonintervention eventually tend to change some patterns of behavior and emotion. The depressed person who does not seek treatment often weathers the storm and the depression lifts. A young child who spits at his siblings will probably, in time, stop spitting. How long these changes will take without intervention is not known. Understanding this, any teacher thinking of implementing a long-term intervention must seriously consider the well-being of the child and all persons connected to that child by way of interaction and relationship. Whether to intervene and how to intervene are ultimately moral choices.

If the decision is made to construct and carry out a long-term intervention, there are five general steps that guide one from analysis to action. We present these steps as basic guidelines, noting that they fit some models of intervention better than others. For instance, a highly rational step-by-step scheme works very nicely within a behavioral approach. In contrast, the psychodynamic and constructivist models tend to be more free-flowing and contextual, often combining the steps listed here into a seamless course of action. The five steps are:

1. Assess the problem.
2. Formulate objectives of intervention.
3. Plan an effective intervention.
4. Implement the intervention.
5. Evaluate the results.

Additionally, as we emphasized in the first chapters discussion of social systems theory, interventions can occur at multiple ecological levels. Many professional programs of intervention simultaneously utilize strategies at different ecological levels.

Assessing the Problem

What's the problem here? How one defines a problem logically influences how one intervenes. The various models of behavior management come into play at this point. Each model views the problem in a different light.

The behavioral model sees the source of the problem in the environmental stimulus or stimuli that reward or promote an individual's negative behavior. Often, though, the concern is not in finding the stimulus that encourages the problem.

Instead, the focus is on finding a stimulus that can be introduced to decrease the negative behavior or increase a positive behavior. Simply, what reward program will modify the behavior? Systematic observations may be recorded in order to count the frequency of the target behavior before, during, and after the intervention period.

The psychodynamic model views a behavior problem as an outward symptom of unresolved, underlying feelings. The problem is primarily the uncomfortable and influential feelings that rumble beneath the surface. Assessment of the situation is twofold: First, professionals utilize insight to interpret these underlying emotions and the relational conflicts that feed the emotions. Second, professionals talk with the child or children to ascertain their understanding of the emotions that fuel their behavior.

The environmental model looks to the way the environmental organization contributes to children's behavior. How does the daily schedule of activities influence behavior? How do aspects of the physical environment encourage or discourage certain behaviors? What are the usual patterns of human interaction, and how do they support or fail to support certain behaviors?

The constructivist model looks at the quality of relationships between the child and important others with a noted emphasis on respectfulness, community, and caring. Of concern within this problem definition are inequalities and conflicts that exist between various participants and the way those inequalities create resentment and negative behavior.

No matter which model one chooses, a clear formulation of the problem is crucial. You may find out later that your assessment was misguided or inaccurate. Remember that behavior management involves trial and error. Nonetheless, a teacher must define the problem first, then develop an intervention plan.

Formulating Objectives of Intervention

Now that you have defined the problem, a new question arises: What change(s) do you want to accomplish through the intervention? Change could take many forms. You could identify a specific behavior that you will try to modify. You may attempt to help a child deal with uncomfortable and difficult feelings. You may try to influence and improve patterns of relationship involving a child or a group. You may attempt to reorganize the daily schedule of activities to promote certain positive changes in one or more children.

As a general rule, it is best to seek relatively modest forms of change. Grandiose plans to refashion groups and individuals into completely new persons often fail miserably. Set simple and realistic goals. Often a plan that begins with the most accessible changes is best.

You should have a clear understanding of the goals or objectives of the intervention. This clarity will help you devise the intervention plan. Additionally, after the intervention has been implemented, you can compare the results to your original intention for purposes of evaluation.

Planning an Effective Intervention

What will you and others do in order to bring about the change(s) you set down in the prior step? Is there a specific order to the actions? Do the actions occur according to a specific scheme of timing? Do different persons bear responsibility for certain aspects of the intervention? The entire plan should be written out in a clear and full form. If the plan involves a sequence of steps, these should be set down before the intervention is initiated.

Part of any plan involves anticipating the final step of this process, the evaluation of effectiveness. Typically, the evaluation demands some form of data regarding the intervention and the progress of the child or children. Behavior modification plans typically require continuous data collection, counting the number of times the target behavior is exhibited. Data collection in the other models may involve qualitative techniques such as journaling or writing field notes detailing daily observations of emotions and behavior. Given the time constraints facing many teachers, this process is often quite informal, relying simply on evaluative conversations between professionals about the outcomes of a given intervention.

Implementing the Intervention

Finally, the plan is put into practice. One important issue in the implementation of one or more interventions regards the question of changing the intervention along the way. Can you change course midstream? Often teachers are midway through the behavior management plan when they realize they were off the mark in the original definition of the problem. Or maybe a different model of intervention suddenly looks more promising than the one initially chosen. Or the child's ecological systems suddenly shift in unexpected and important ways.

Can you change midstream? There is no absolute answer to this question. Traditional behavior modification may call for a full trial of the intervention, including accurate data collection, so that the effects may be scientifically evaluated. Despite this tradition, may talented professionals have developed the skills to alter and adapt their interventions on the fly. Doing so is no easy task; it requires sensitive and skilled judgment. This sort of adeptness and flexibility is probably less common among new practitioners of behavior management techniques.

Evaluating the Results

What are the results of the intervention? The short story involves a simple judgment about improvement or deterioration. Did things get better or worse? To what extent was the objective met? Additionally, we must be aware that interventions do not merely influence individuals and groups in ways that we anticipated. Unexpected and novel changes in behavior, emotion, and relationship come about. In fact, an intervention might solve one problem and create a new one. Attention to these subtleties is important in conducting a full evaluation.

As stated earlier, evaluation often relies on data that are collected during the actual implementation of the intervention. These data may be quantitative, such as counts of behaviors or scores on behavior rating scales. The data may be qualitative, including journals and observational field notes. Additionally, new data may be gathered during the evaluation process. Interview the child or children whose behavior was at the center of the problem. Often the child or children know best whether improvement has occurred. Interview important peers or other adults who are in a position to know. Data may be gathered from many persons.

Central to the evaluation is some determination of how and why the intervention produced the results. If you can understand how the intervention influenced the child or children, then new interventions (if necessary) will be easier to design. You will have important knowledge about what is effective or ineffective with this child or group.

We should view this final step of the long-term intervention process either as terminal or as naturally leading into the first step for another round of analysis and intervention. If the behavior problems have been solved to the satisfaction of child, teacher, parents, and others, then the process is completed. If the negative behavior or social conflict persists, or if new problems arise, then the information gathered in this final step can lead naturally back to step 1 and a new definition of the problem at hand.

EXAMINING A CASE

We have just outlined a general process for both immediate and long-term intervention, attempting to provide some guidelines and direction while acknowledging the need for flexibility and innovation within the specific problem situation. This book is founded on the premise that teachers and other professionals working with children can improve behavior management skills by practicing on narrative cases of problem situations. By reading, analyzing, and discussing cases, the reader can begin to think seriously and carefully about the many possible intervention options. The cases in this book are not presented as puzzles that can be solved once and for all. They are open and exploratory, allowing for a breadth of thoughtful analysis instead of the simplicity of cookbook schemes.

In the following section, we present an initial case and provide an example of how one might develop both an immediate intervention and a long-term intervention. We present long-term interventions that draw from each of the models of behavior management (behavioral, psychodynamic, environmental, constructivist) covered in chapter 1. The case example, titled "I Don't Like Mondays," demonstrates the basic structure and style of the cases offered in the remainder of the book. First, we briefly describe an incident of problem behavior. Then, a longer section delves into pertinent background information about the child(ren), the teacher(s) or adult(s), and the setting in which the incident took place. We provide this background information to emphasize how knowledge of the relationships and events preceding the actual incident are crucial to case analysis and intervention design. The incident itself is only the point of entry into deeper social issues and problems.

CASE EXAMPLE: "I DON'T LIKE MONDAYS"

Incident

As Willie entered the room, he rushed to his desk, sat himself down with a loud commotion, and remarked, "I don't like Mondays. Just another day of crap for my brain." On his desk lay five math worksheets that he was to work on during homeroom period because he had failed to turn them in the Friday before. Willie knew that he would never complete these five worksheets in the time (10 minutes) allotted and besides, he hated math.

Ms. Simmons, trying to ignore his initial comments, thought to herself, "Jeez, not another bad Monday with Willie." Ms. Simmons knew that weekends were always rough on Willie.

As the other children entered the room, Tommy approached Willie, threw a baseball cap at him, and remarked, "Found this in the hallway. Next time I'll flush it down the toilet." As Susan squeezed by Willie's desk, she accidentally brushed up against him.

Willie remarked, "Get your fat ass out of my face."

Tommy replied, "You love it."

"Only with your mama," quipped Willie.

"In your dreams, hat boy," cracked Tommy. He reached out his hand and tapped the visor of Willie's baseball cap. Willie grabbed Tommy's arm. Tommy tried to pull away.

"Gentlemen!" Ms. Simmons called from the front of the room. Willie released Tommy's arm and flashed a too-compliant smile at his teacher. Tommy grumbled and fixed his ruffled shirtsleeve. Three seconds later, once Ms. Simmons's vigilant eyes had dropped back to the paperwork on her desk, Willie dived across his desk and grabbed Tommy by the throat. He pushed Tommy up against the wall and started pounding him in the stomach. By the time Ms. Simmons reached them, the two boys were engaged in a full fistfight.

Background Information

This scene occurred during the 10-minute homeroom period at the start of a Monday morning in Chester Burnett Senior High School, a large public school in an urban area. Burnett High is located in a racially mixed, economically poor neighborhood filled with symbols of both hope and misery. Boarded-up windows and tenement buildings line the street where the school is located. Almost surprisingly, on the corner are two new businesses, a grocery store owned by a Pakistani family and a small coffee shop that serves two eggs, coffee, and toast for a dollar fifty-nine. Unfortunately, around the corner is the most financially successful business in the neighborhood, a crack house where buyers and users come and go at all hours.

The student body of Burnett High reflects the local neighborhood: 55% African-American, 28% Latin-American, and the rest Anglo-American or new immigrants from Eastern Europe or India. Burnett High School has a graduation rate of 60%. This is an increase over previous years. A new school principal has provided the needed spark, rallying old and new faculty members to overhaul an outdated curriculum and try some innovative programs. For example, Burnett High School now has an entire department of service learning staffed by three new teachers. These teachers work closely with a wide variety of local groups and agencies to bring students into nearby neighborhoods for purposes of improving the community. Students are given high school credit for work tasks ranging from serving sandwiches in a soup kitchen to learning computer skills at a local bank.

Ms. Julia Simmons has taught home economics and English in this inner-city school district for more than 25 years. As an experienced teacher of streetwise kids, Julia Simmons will tell you that she has seen many boys like Willie over the years. Some have gone on to do well. Too many have not. She speaks frequently and wearily of retirement, that final rest for the teacher who has undoubtedly earned a break. Yet in the same breath, this veteran teacher remarks that she really wants to make a difference in the lives of her students. That's when her eyes twinkle with the same enthusiasm that brought her to this job many years ago. Julia often reminisces about how the school was a better place in the old days; no guns, no drugs—especially no drugs.

Now cramped into a small room behind the library with old desks crammed side-by-side, Julia does her best to keep the students under control. Julia's teaching style is a paradoxical mix of frustrated punitiveness and gentle, genuine caring. She has a saying in her room: "I walk quietly and carry a big stick." Unfortunately for her students, it means that the punishment for their inappropriate acts often far exceeds the significance of the act itself. On the other hand, Julia has been known to go out of her way to help her students, even bringing in clothing and food from home to give to those in financial need. Additionally, when not overstressed, Julia is a generous and supportive listener.

Although Tommy is one of the top students in the sophomore class, Ms. Simmons suspects that his shiny wrapper is cleaner than his contents. Occasionally, she has seen him in the hallway, whispering and gossiping among some of the tougher boys. He hangs around with a group who are frequently arrested for small-scale drug-dealing. Tommy has no police record. He never seems to get in any trouble, on the streets or in school, but he doesn't appear completely innocent. Ms. Simmons has wondered if Tommy doesn't instigate and promote some of the conflicts she sees. She knows he is highly intelligent. She wonders if he is smart enough to be conniving and slippery. In her more creative moments, Ms. Simmons imagines that Tommy is the gangster boss behind the scenes, arranging everything in such a way that he gets away scot-free. Having no direct evidence of any wrongdoing, Ms. Simmons keeps a tense but polite distance from Tommy. She and Tommy have never really exchanged anything more than a "good morning."

This was not the first time Willie had started a fight. He had been suspended from school on several other occasions. Willie is a tough kid with tattoos and scars covering his body that prove his manhood. Only 15, he's already lived a lifetime of torment and suffering.

Willie lives in the section of town known as "Bangtown." This area got its name from the gang fights, drugs, and violence that have occurred there since the rise of crack sales in the 1980s. Willie was born to Lucia Greer when she was just 17 years old. Lucia did not know much about caring for herself, let alone a new baby. Consequently, Willie grew up relying on himself to get things done. He learned early how to make his own breakfast, how to get around town, and most of all, how to defend himself. Lucia had dated many men after Willie was born, but none stayed longer than a few months. The latest boyfriend, Victor, had been with Lucia for about a year. For Lucia it was a stable relationship, but for Willie it was a series of beatings that usually culminated on weekends as Victor celebrated the end of the work week by partying from Friday evening to Sunday. During this time, Willie did his best to avoid Victor by hiding in his bedroom, but Victor would typically visit Willie to reaffirm his dominance in the house. Fortunately for Willie, Victor worked the night shift during the week and their schedules prevented much contact. This past weekend it was no different. When Willie played the TV or his music too loud, it was Victor who came to tell him to turn it down. If Willie wasn't so stubborn, he might have avoided many of the arguments. But Victor, who was usually drunk, would yell at Willie for only a short time before he would use his hands to resolve the disagreement.

Lucia, who worked 50 to 60 hours a week, never really knew what was going on. When she came home on most nights, Willie was usually sleeping and Victor was usually passed out on the sofa.

Lucia knew that Willie was a difficult child and that school was tough for him. He had difficulties in learning to read. He couldn't get along with the other students. He flew off the handle at the slightest provocation. By the fourth grade, he had already lost interest in school. Lucia could relate to this because she too had difficulty in school and eventually dropped out when she was 15 years old. As she watched her son grow up, Lucia saw him go through periods of deep depression. His chronic unhappiness was difficult for her to bear. Sometimes she felt an overwhelming sense of guilt, as if it must be all her fault.

Julia Simmons knows Willie and Lucia well. She has spent evenings on the telephone with Lucia discussing Willie; his behavior, his academics, and his future. Julia often discusses Willie's problems in depth with him before school. But Willie is cautious never to mention the beatings that he receives at home. He feels great shame that Victor beats him.

Immediate Intervention

If possible, Willie and Tommy must be separated. Safety is a major consideration. Certainly, the teacher can firmly tell the boys to break it up. Yet she must also make a quick decision about whether her safety or the safety of any students will be compromised by her physical intervention. Should she jump in to separate the combatants? She must decide quickly. If she is unable to stop the fight, she will need to clear the other students out of the room and call for help if possible. Given Ms. Simmons's age and the size of these two adolescent boys, we can envision her directing the boys very firmly to stop while simultaneously moving other students out of the room. She sends a reliable student to the office to retrieve the personnel necessary (assistant principal, school police officer, etc.) to pull the boys apart.

Once the fight is over, the combatants will need to be removed from the class and separated from each other. Removing Willie and Tommy from the situation would let them cool down and allow the class to return to peace and order so that learning can resume. Julia Simmons has a strong relationship with Willie. Once he calms down, it would be ideal if she could be the one to talk him through the entire sequence of events, discussing both his feelings and his behavior. Because this teacher does not have much trust built up with Tommy, it may be best for someone who knows Tommy better to talk to him.

Long-Term Intervention

The conflict described in the case requires not only immediate action but a careful plan of long-term intervention to prevent similar incidents from occurring in the future. Given Willie's history of fighting in school and Ms. Simmons's suspicion that Tommy may be a prominent instigator of conflicts, such a plan makes sense. In this section, we will generate long-term intervention options using each of the four models. Typically, however, a long-term intervention will involve only one, two, or perhaps three models.

Psychodynamic Model

According to the psychodynamic model, Willie's violent behavior acts out some very powerful underlying feelings. An incident such as this is viewed as a crucial opportunity for learning, a chance for a caring and skilled adult to guide a young person through powerful emotions to self-knowledge. Anger seems to be the most obvious emotion, but we can also anticipate that Willie may feel sadness, jealousy, a personal sense of inadequacy, or rejection. Assessment and intervention will involve talking with Willie to help him express, understand, and find more constructive ways of handling those feelings. This process involves the development of an intimate form of trust between student and teacher. In this regard, we can see that the psychodynamic model of intervention does not rely on one-shot cures but involves the gradual development of a therapeutic relationship over time. It is possible that Willie should be referred to a qualified psychotherapist for ongoing therapy.

Through the conversation, Ms. Simmons wants to guide and support Willie to develop a greater understanding of his own emotions, the source of those emotions, and the way he expresses those emotions in physical violence. She ultimately wants to help him to look closely at ways of handling his feelings that do not involve violence. Additionally, Ms. Simmons is aware that Willie tends to seem emotionally unsteady on Mondays. She suspects that something negative is happening at home on the weekends. If a moment arises in her conversation when Willie seems to be trusting her and looking to her for guidance, she will tell him her observations and ask him if anything is going on at home. She must be aware that this is a very delicate question that is very likely to raise his defenses.

Two specific issues concerning Tommy must be addressed. First, Tommy's feelings and actions must be taken into consideration. From the teasing through the fight itself, he was a full participant in this incident. A trusted and qualified professional (guidance counselor? teacher?) should talk to Tommy privately about this incident and his feelings toward and relationship with Willie. He needs to become aware of the connection between his feelings toward Willie and the way he treated Willie. Additionally, given the way Tommy hangs around with a criminal crowd in the hallways, he may already be involved in delinquent activity. His affiliation with a negative crowd should be questioned and even challenged. We can envision a trusted adult asking Tommy serious questions like, "What do you want for your future? Why do you hang around with the kids who deal drugs?" These are very personal and confrontational questions. If they are to be asked, they must be asked by an adult whom Tommy views as caring, as acting in his best interests. If these questions are merely thrown at Tommy in an accusatory fashion by someone whom Tommy does not trust, he is not likely to view the intervention as helpful. He is likely to defend himself, hide his activities, and continue down a bad path.

Environmental Model

There are clear indications that some academic tasks are experienced as boring or frustrating by Willie. He describes the school day as "another load of crap for my brain." He has failed to complete his math work from the day before. This makes us wonder what personal interests he has and how these can be connected to the curriculum to make the work more personally meaningful. We need to talk to him about this. We may need to talk to his math teacher to find out more about Willie's performance in that class. Is he frustrated? Is he keeping up with the work? Does he need tutoring or other support?

In regard to the physical layout of the classroom during homeroom period, maybe Willie and Tommy should not sit near each other, at least until the heated emotions settle. Additionally, we wonder if the physical distance between Ms. Simmons and her students is too great. She may have greater influence if her desk is not so far removed from the students' desks.

Socially, it is obvious that the relationship between the two boys is tense and conflict-ridden. It might be best to sit them down with Ms. Simmons and discuss their differences and gripes. Additionally, given the cliquish nature of teenage peer groups, we should investigate whether the friction between Willie and Tommy is indicative of larger conflicts between groups of friends. It is very possible that a clash between two groups of peers or within a single group is playing out in the form of a one-on-one fight. This can be investigated by talking to the two boys, talking to other students, and asking the advice of other teachers who keep close track of the networks of friendships among the various students.

Constructivist Model

In this model, Ms. Simmons would view the fight as a sign that the unity, respect, and caring among students in the class (and perhaps in the school more broadly) needs to be studied, discussed, and improved. The classroom network of relationships, the intimate community of students, is failing in a significant way. A fight is viewed as a conflict between the two boys involved and as a classroom community issue that impacts and involves all.

Ms. Simmons might first reflect on her own role, examining the way she is talking to and treating her students. Is she living up to her value of reciprocal respect? She must look at the ways that, despite her best intentions, she is not supporting or encouraging respectful and equal relationships between students. Her questioning, in particular, should focus on her relationships with and her effect on the two boys involved in the fight.

Because the violence has threatened and disrupted the classroom community, Ms. Simmons may want Willie (and perhaps Tommy) to receive some sort of consequences that are closely related to the offense. Most likely, she will bring up this issue for discussion among all the students in the class. The act of opening up the issue for discussion encourages ownership and responsibility among all the students.

The discussion of the incident among the entire class should be orderly but open. One person speaks at a time. All voices are honored and encouraged. All must speak in respectful ways. The discussion has a bit of a New England town meeting feel to it. The teacher facilitates, guiding the conversation gently toward a conclusion that produces unity and allows the group to continue to work in safety and comfort.

What might be said in such a group meeting is not known. The goal is to help the students inquire seriously about the ongoing conflicts and general weaknesses in their web of relationships. The discussion might be emotional. Ms. Simmons may wish to bring in a guidance counselor or other supportive professional who is trusted by these students. The discussion must be practical and constructive, leading ultimately to a group decision on specific actions for improvement. During this process, Ms. Simmons must remain open to the fact that the students may comment on or critique specific things she has done. They may claim she is unfair or too controlling. They may criticize other aspects of their school. If the teacher can open herself up to this process as a chance to learn about herself and to learn how to better meet the needs of her students, then she can benefit from the students' words of criticism.

Behavioral Model

The most likely use of the behavioral model would be a functional analysis of the classroom variables that promote the negative behavior, both Willie's assault on Tommy and Tommy's teasing. Such an analysis would only be possible if the negative behaviors in question (assault, teasing) are fairly common for these two boys. Although we have some suspicion that the conflict between Tommy and Willie is ongoing, we have no evidence in this case that these two specific behaviors are being exhibited frequently by these boys. For this reason, a functional analysis does not seem to be a likely choice. The use of a behavioral contract through which one or both of these boys earns privileges or rewards may be appropriate.

Summary of Case Analysis

Based primarily on the psychodynamic, environmental, and constructivist models, we can quickly summarize our case analysis using the five general steps detailed earlier.

1. *Assess the problem.* The surface problem seems to be a heated personal conflict between Tommy and Willy. This relational difficulty is probably the tip of a number of larger icebergs. It is likely that both Tommy and Willie are going through some personal struggles of their own. Willie's family situation involving the abuse by his mother's boyfriend is painful for him. Tommy's apparent criminal activity is a growing problem for him. Additionally, as a broader ecological issue, we are aware that some between-group or within-group struggles may be occurring among networks of peers. All these hypotheses require additional investigation, but we are pretty sure that discussions with Tommy and Willie will bring many of the details of these three background "icebergs" to light.

2. *Formulate objectives of intervention.* For the surface issue concerning the conflict between Tommy and Willie, our goal is to help these boys learn to handle interpersonal difficulties without fighting. In regard to the three "icebergs" (Willie's family problems; Tommy's apparent criminal activities; apparent group conflicts in the larger student body), our goal is to find out if these suspected problems are really serious, if these issues really require some sort of intervention.

3. *Plan an effective intervention.*

    a. *Willie.* Individual Life Space Intervention or brief counseling session with trusted, qualified professional (Ms. Simmons).

    b. *Tommy.* Individual Life Space Intervention or brief counseling session with trusted, qualified professional (guidance counselor? teacher?).

    c. *Tommy and Willie.* Possible combined counseling session to discuss conflicts and work out differences.

    d. *Ms. Simmons's Homeroom.* Class discussion led by Ms. Simmons and guidance counselor about how to improve unity and cooperation in the group.

4. *Implement the intervention.*

5. *Evaluate the results.* Two to three weeks after the interventions have been completed, Ms. Simmons should meet with both boys individually and

together to evaluate the effectiveness of the interventions. What has happened? Have the two boys fought with each other or anyone else? How are the two boys getting along with each other? What is the status of the "iceberg" issues? Ms. Simmons (and perhaps other school personnel) should monitor both the surface issue (Tommy and Willie's relationship) and the iceberg issues on a regular basis. Observing student behavior in class and in the hallways and holding discussions with various students about these issues will allow these professionals to keep a finger on the pulse of these problems.

REFERENCES

Danforth, S. (1997). Autobiography as critical pedagogy: Locating myself in class-based oppression. *Teaching Education, 9*(1), 3–14.

Harrington, H. L., Quinn-Leering, K., & Hodson, L. (1996). Written case analyses and critical reflection. *Teaching and Teacher Education, 12*(1), 25–37.

Wood, M. M., & Long, N. J. (1991). *Life Space Intervention*. Austin, TX: PRO-ED.

PART II

BEHAVIOR MANAGEMENT CASES

CASE 1

BLINDED BY SCIENCE

THE INCIDENT

As Charlie Jameson sat in science class that May morning, the last thing that he heard before passing out was a loud "thump." The "thump" that Charlie heard was Rashon Rickson's science textbook hitting him on the head.

Rashon had worked for the previous two weeks to develop a model of the Mars *Pathfinder,* along with a working model of the rover. The model, built to scale, included Martian-looking rocks, one with the name "Barnacle Bill." In a matter of minutes, Rashon's exacting work was scattered to pieces on the ground with Charlie towering over the mess like a giant who had just destroyed a miniature village. Unable to speak, Rashon just stared in amazement. His lower lip quivered with sadness. Meanwhile, Charlie looked on and let out a bellowing laugh. As his laugh echoed within Rashon's ears, Rashon's face slowly became red with anger. Charlie then very calmly took his seat and began to finish up his own project. Seething with anger, Rashon grabbed his science textbook, walked up behind Charlie's desk, and with all his weight slammed it on Charlie's head. As Charlie fell to the ground, Mr. Saxton, the science teacher, ran to grab him, but missed and instead landed on the pile of children who had gathered around. Mr. Saxton was visibly shaken by the incident. Ordering children back to their desks while simultaneously grabbing Rashon by the arm, Mr. Saxton's entire body was quaking.

"Jay, go to the office and tell Mr. Griffin to call an ambulance, and tell him to get down here. Now!" Mr. Saxton barked to the student closest to the door.

BACKGROUND INFORMATION

It wasn't the first time that Charlie and Rashon had been involved in an altercation and possibly wouldn't be the last. Charlie was the class bully. Everyone—the students in the class, the teachers in the school, and the principal—kept an eye out for Charlie. Charlie's sheer size made him stand out in this fifth-grade class. He would intimidate any child who stood in his way. Charlie was the boss of the students and often got his way through a threatening glance. Charlie was too familiar with the in-school-suspension (ISS) procedures and did not fear being sent home for hitting or fighting. Charlie's dad, Henry "Rock" Jameson, had instilled in his son the desire to use whatever it took to be a "winner" in life. Charlie was often heard telling his victims, "Suckers like you make up the losers in the world."

According to most kids in the class, Rashon was a "geek." He was a good-looking fifth grader, but his glasses and his sweater vests often made him look like the professor's son. Rashon's interest in science led him to spend long hours searching the Internet and prevented him from socializing with other students. In fact, he could make an exact replica of the *Pathfinder* because he was able to study pictures from the various Web sites that kept him apprised of the latest developments from the Mars landing. Rashon was the most intelligent child in class, often out-smarting Mr. Saxton. Rashon was also one of the most despised kids, because he flaunted his intelligence and money. Every time he won a trophy, he would proudly walk around the room placing it in the faces of his losing competitors. For Rashon, winning intellectual endeavors validated his worth. Extremely competitive, his parents were often more proud of his accolades than the actual projects. His dad, Zachary Rickson, a computer systems manager at a high-tech firm, paid little atten-tion to Rashon except when he brought home a prize. His mother often had little time to spend with Rashon because her career required that she work many evenings and weekends. A millionaire real-estate agent, Tina Rickson was always after the next property, the next client, the next deal.

Why Rashon didn't fear Charlie was a mystery. Rashon was Charlie's antithesis in life and mixing the two often resulted in Rashon's ripped clothes and Charlie's satisfied glow. Oddly enough, in a number of ways Charlie and Rashon were a lot alike. Both had parents who valued competitiveness and cherished winning. Both boys learned that it was primarily after some incident (Charlie's fights and Rashon's trophies) that their parents would take the time to acknowledge and talk to them.

On the morning of the above incident, Rashon and his father were eating breakfast together. As on most mornings, his mom was already at the office. The father and son did not talk. Rashon ate cereal while reading a science book, and Zachary drank his cappuccino while tapping away on a laptop computer. Each was busy living in his own little world until Rashon had an accident. He was pouring milk on his second bowl of cereal when it spilled. The milk made a quick path to Zachary's laptop.

"What are you doing? Do you know the damage liquids can do to this com-puter?" Zachary shouted. Zachary had been up most of the night working on a computer program, and it might have been his fatigue that caused him to "snap out" at Rashon. Rashon grabbed for a towel and tried to soak up the milk while pleading for his father's forgiveness. Zachary continued to yell. Then something odd hap-pened. Normally, by now Rashon would be in tears from his father's scolding, but on this day Rashon fought back the tears and yelled at his father.

"All that you care about is your damn computer!" he shouted as he bolted out the door. Zachary called him back, realizing that there was some truth to his state-ment, but it was too late; he was gone.

In another part of town another father-son scenario was playing out in the Jameson household. At breakfast, Charlie and his father, Rock, got into an argument.

Rock was angry with Charlie because Charlie stole cigarettes from his coat and smoked them in the basement. Rock actually hadn't caught Charlie smoking, but he had found cigarette butts behind the furnace. As he yelled at Charlie during breakfast, the boy's tears fell into his cereal. Despite the overwhelming evidence, Charlie denied the allegations. His denials only intensified Rock's anger until he finally slapped Charlie on the face.

Rock loved his son, but he often used the same tough disciplinary methods that his father had used on him. He used punishment to solve most of his family problems. As Charlie ran out the door that morning, he told his father that he hated him and that he wished he were dead. Rock felt bad and yelled for his son, but it was too late for apologies. Charlie had already pedaled his bike out of sight.

"Damn, another time that I screwed up," Rock mumbled under his breath.

CASE 2

GETTING CAUGHT

THE INCIDENT

As Mr. Conners, the teacher in the self-contained behavior disorders (BD) class at Stewart High School, sits at his desk busily grading papers, his students are hard at work at their desks. David and Tommy are sitting next to each other discussing how attractive Susie is looking in her provocative, pink sweater.

"Boy, I'd like to get me some of that," Tommy remarks to David.

David agrees and says to Tommy, "Watch this!" David then moves up two seats so that he is now seated directly behind Susie. After giving Tommy a smirk, he whispers in Susie's ear, "I can't wait to squeeze your love melons." He then tells her that he plans to follow her home to get some "action." "Don't worry, no one will ever see us," he adds. Having been a victim of sexual abuse in the past, Susie becomes very frightened and immediately runs to Mr. Conners's desk to tell him about David's comments. Mr. Conners immediately turns around and glares at David, who is now back in his original seat.

David looks up and in a surprised voice says, "What?"

"In the hall," Mr. Conners calls out.

As David walks toward the door, Tommy laughs and calls out, "You're busted." In the hall, Mr. Conners confronts David about the incident. Mr. Conners fires a series of questions, one after the other, but David denies each one and then begins to cry. Through his tears he is heard to say, "Everyone hates me" and "I never get a fair shake."

BACKGROUND INFORMATION

David is a tall, good-looking young man who has been in and out of residential treatment centers and special schools for the past 5 years. Now 16, he has been in Mr. Conners's self-contained BD classroom for 3 months. His entry into Mr. Conners's room did not come easy for David. It was only after his educational advocate, Billy Russo, pleaded for him to be moved to a less restrictive environment that David was placed in Mr. Conners's classroom. His prior placement was in the Central Behavioral Center (CBC), a center that provides a very tight structure for students with severe behavioral problems.

The CBC uses a "level system" for behavior management, with level 1 being the most restrictive and level 7 the least restrictive. Students who enter are placed on level 2 (level 1 is a punishment level) and must earn their way upward to level 7 to gain entry to a self-contained behavior disorders class in a local public school in the Woodward School District. During each period of the day, students are awarded 5 points for appropriate social behavior. If the student earns 55 or more points for the day and continues this for 10 school days, that student advances to the next highest level.

David had been attending the CBC for the past 2 years. What expedited his move was the work of Billy Russo. While at the CBC, David had earned his way up to level 4, despite falling back to lower levels at times. When Mr. Russo was assigned to David by the state of Wisconsin, David had just earned his level 4 status. As his educational advocate, Mr. Russo immediately went to the CBC to meet David, speak to his teachers, and tour the center. Mr. Russo came away from this initial meeting feeling very concerned about David. Mr. Russo felt that in David's case the CBC's behavioral system was ineffective, possibly doing more harm than good. After several follow-up visits, Mr. Russo finally persuaded the staff at the CBC to place David in a self-contained classroom at Stewart High School for a trial period of 3 months. The staff from the CBC was reluctant, but under the threat of a "due process" by Mr. Russo, they agreed to the trial period. Mr. Conners, present at the meeting, was also reluctant to bend the rules for David, but under pressure from his supervisor agreed to the trial period.

It is important to note that at this meeting, David's CBC teacher, Jan Hallson, brought up three prior incidents in her classroom where David displayed inappropriate behavior. In the first incident, when David was wrestling with two other students, one being a young woman, David was accused of grabbing her in her "private" parts. David said it was an accident and that he meant nothing by it. In another situation, David was accused of sending one of his teachers love notes. The notes had sexual overtones and Ms. Kackasaw, the teacher, viewed it as a "schoolboy crush." David, however, was devastated when Ms. Kackasaw finally confronted him and told him to stop sending her notes. Listless, David did not perform well in school during the month that followed. Finally, in a third incident, David was accused of downloading pornography from the Internet at school. Although no one observed David doing this, many teachers felt that he was one of the few children in the school who was knowledgeable enough to commit such an act. In addition, Ms. Hallson overheard her students discussing how David had downloaded "dirty" pictures. She confronted David, but he denied involvement in the incident.

In addition to David's behavior, at the placement meeting David's social worker, Raine Tuttle, was quick to mention David's deteriorating home life. From the records, Raine indicated, David lives with his mother in a single-family home. David's father had left the household when David was 10 after a series of incidents of physical and sexual abuse. Raine claimed that David's mother had thrown the father out of the house after a drunken episode in which he broke David's arm.

Raine also pointed out that David's mom is currently having a lot of difficulty with David. Apparently, David has twice run away from home and does not adhere to his mother's curfew of 11 o'clock. When his mother confronts him about his behavior David often states that now he is the "man of the house."

Three months have passed since that placement decision. The scenario documented in this case is David's first major behavioral incident, although David has displayed minor behavior problems since being placed in Mr. Conners's room. For instance, almost daily David complains that his class work is too difficult for him, despite the fact that he performed quite well on a number of standardized achievement tests. David has also been involved in two loud arguments, both involving another student calling him names. One time David was caught carving his name into a desk with a knife. Although Mr. Conners claims that David is not much of a problem compared to the eight other students in the class, he still feels that David has much improvement to make before he can be mainstreamed in regular education classes. Mr. Conners notes that David displays a pattern whereby he has a number of days of excellent behavior interrupted by a day or two of unruly and disruptive behavior.

CASE 3

PEOPLE CHANGE

THE INCIDENT

As Vito rolled down the hall in his wheelchair, he felt the eyes of his classmates watching him. Some students stopped talking and stared at him like motorists moving past an automobile accident. A few students called, "Hey, Vito." When Vito reached his destination, biology class, Mr. Cronwell greeted him with a cheery "Hello," but Vito did not reply. Instead, he moved to his special desk, the one without the chair, and watched his fellow students file into the room. As the second bell rang, the last few students hurriedly found their desks. Taking her seat next to Vito, Susan whispered "hello" to Vito.

Immediately, Vito exploded with a series of expletives and angry statements: "Don't talk to me. You're just like the rest of 'em. I don't need your pity." With all eyes now fixed on him, Vito looked around and said, "Screw all of you." With that comment he quickly moved his wheelchair into the aisle and headed for the door.

Mr. Cronwell quickly positioned himself between Vito and the door. Intercepting Vito, Mr. Cronwell empathetically said, "Look, Vito, the kids are just trying to be nice."

Vito, who was becoming increasingly angrier, shouted out, "I don't want your niceness or pity or help." As Mr. Cronwell escorted Vito through the door and into the hallway, he again pleaded with Vito to calm down and keep his voice down, but Vito refused and shouted, "Kiss my ass!" as he wheeled down the hall. Mr. Cronwell just watched and shook his head, thinking to himself how much Vito had changed over the past 8 months.

BACKGROUND INFORMATION

A high school sports hero, Vito is now only a semblance of his former glory. He was the captain of the football team and one of the school's fastest athletes in track. He was also a scholar-athlete who excelled in his English and science classes. He was always on the honor roll. But now he has trouble learning new information that is abstract in nature. He was a popular student who would light up the room upon entering it. Now he sours the happy moods and either speaks with spite to others or refuses to talk at all. This drastic change in Vito came about because of "the accident."

One late November night, Vito's parents, Debbie and Frank, received the phone call that all parents dread. It was from a police officer who was calling to tell them that Vito had been in a terrible accident. As his parents hurriedly dressed and rushed to the hospital, Debbie's first thought was about Vito's heavy drinking. Vito began drinking and experimenting with illegal drugs when he was 15. Now two years later his drinking binges were occurring more frequently. Vito's athleticism and personality made him a popular person to invite to parties. Unfortunately, Vito's mix of drugs and alcohol made a dangerous combination. On that particular night, Vito went out with friends to celebrate the team's latest victory. As he gave his mom a hug before leaving, Debbie had an uneasy feeling. Like other parents their age, Debbie and Frank felt that drinking and getting drunk was just part of growing up. Both Debbie and Frank drank on weekends when they were in high school and, although it was a bit unnerving, they saw no harm in Vito's celebrations. How things have changed. Debbie now coordinates the local Mothers Against Drunk Driving group and Frank works with the local after-school program that provides midnight basketball for youth.

The vehicle that was driven by a drunken friend smashed into a tree and Vito went headfirst through the windshield. He was the most seriously injured of the group. Miraculously, his friends Ned, Matt, and Pete only suffered minor injuries. At first, it was "touch and go" as Vito spent 2 weeks in a coma while hooked up to life support. It took 3 full months in rehabilitation before Vito was well enough to be sent home.

After 3 months in intense rehabilitation, Vito emerged a different person. By that time many of his friendships had waned and his attitude had soured. He had many sleepless nights when he would ask himself, "Why should I live?" Despite having a large group of friends, Vito often felt ashamed when they visited him. There were quite a few days when Vito refused to see any visitors.

Before long, Vito's mother was talking to him about going back to school. After a series of evaluations, it was determined that Vito required speech therapy because of his facial reconstructive surgery and some consultation services from the special education teacher, Martha Pearson, because of his head injury. According to Martha, "Whatever Vito did poorly prior to the accident, he will now probably perform worse." She understood how head injuries often amplify the weaker cognitive ability areas to make them worse. In Vito's case, his occasional bouts of depression before the accident now became more frequent and more pronounced. In addition to these problems, he also suffered a spinal cord injury resulting in the loss of use of his legs and restricting him to a wheelchair.

When Vito started back to school a month ago, some 7 months after the accident, he received a lot of support from teachers and students. In fact, he was actually embarrassed by all the attention that he received. Because he tired easily, he started back to school on a part-time basis. On most days, he was permitted to go to the nurse's office to take short naps. Although his friends tried not to treat him differently, things had undoubtedly changed. Vito could not attend physical education classes or play sports. He used the school's elevator to get to his classes. Vito's fatigue also prevented him from participating in many of the after-school programs. Worst of all, Vito could not go out with his friends as he used to. He and his friends were now restricted to his house or neighborhood. Through all these changes, Vito tried to remain optimistic, but over time, his new limitations began to take their toll on him. He became sullen and bitter about his life and his relationships. He felt that he had lost everything he loved about his life. He felt overwhelmed by hopelessness and anger.

WHEN IS COLLABORATION NOT COLLABORATION?

THE INCIDENT

"Boring, boring," was Stanley's reply to Mr. Gaskins's question.

"Let me ask you again," Mr. Gaskins repeated. "In this experiment, what happened when we put water in a bottle and placed it in the freezer?"

"The damn thing blew up," Stanley shot back.

"No, that's not the answer I am looking for and don't use that language in this class," Mr. Gaskins replied. With his comment, Stanley laid his head back down on his desk and closed his eyes. Out of aggravation, Mr. Gaskins walked up to Stanley's desk, laid his hand on his shoulder, and whispered in his ear, "Get out of my class."

Familiar with the procedure, Stanley grabbed his coat and knapsack, and, stomping his feet, left the room. Thelma Lawson, the co-teacher in this eighth-grade inclusive science class, ran after him. By the time she finally caught up to Stanley, he was angrily calling Mr. Gaskins a "mean old *$#!*."

"Stanley," said Ms. Lawson as she put her hand on his shoulder, "you have to give it some effort if you hope to remain in mainstream science." Stanley wasn't certain that he wanted to remain in Mr. Gaskins's science class and, in fact, enjoyed last year when Ms. Lawson taught him in her special education science.

"I learned so much from you," Stanley pleaded.

"I know that you did, but this year the principal has decided to change to collaborative teaching in inclusive classes. We're trying to get rid of segregated programs," Ms. Lawson explained in return. "Look, Stanley, let's think about what happened today," Ms. Lawson counseled. "When you came into science class, you walked through the doors laughing, and then you slammed your bag down on the table. Next, you continued to talk to Sheena, even after the bell rang. Finally, halfway through Mr. Gaskins's introduction, you plopped your head down on the table and closed your eyes." Throughout Ms. Lawson's analysis, Stanley stared at the ground, motionless, and said nothing. "Well, what do you think you could have done differently?" she asked.

"The man is an old fool and his classes are boring," Stanley answered. Ms. Lawson smiled at his response because she knew that, in part, his answer was correct.

✒ Background Information

As she questioned Stanley's behavior, Ms. Lawson knew that Mr. Gaskins was a very old-fashioned teacher who hated collaboration because it meant that the so-called "troubled kids" (i.e., those with learning disabilities, behavior disorders, and developmental disabilities) were now placed back in his class. Mr. Gaskins had worked hard to pass students with whom he was having problems to special education. Thelma saw Mr. Gaskins teach and felt sorry for the students. She knew that her hands were tied because, despite this being a collaborative class, her role was relegated to grading papers, assisting students, and helping Mr. Gaskins set up decades-old science experiments. Mr. Gaskins was quite open and honest with Thelma in telling her that he did not want to teach collaboratively and that he did not want those troubled kids in his class. He openly admitted to her that all that he wanted to do was do his job the way he knew how without any changes in his classroom.

For Thelma, who was new to the school, his attitude was far from what she wanted to hear. She had worked for the past 3 years in the elementary school, just minutes away, and was brought on board because the principal, John Make, had been looking for someone in special education who could work with teachers like Mr. Gaskins. In fact, the running joke at Franklin Middle School was, "When is collaboration not collaboration? When you work with Mr. Gaskins." Thelma was a shining star at the elementary school, and her work in making the elementary school a collaborative environment had been the primary reason why John worked hard to recruit her for his school.

An inner-city school, Franklin City Middle School is located between an abandoned warehouse and the Guzzle and Go Liquor Store. It's not uncommon to see adults selling booze to underage youths who hang out near the store. For the youths, a few extra dollars to the adult usually secures their purchases. The high dropout rate in the district, which until recently mainly affected only the high school, was now being felt in the middle school. A lack of money for supplies and a lack of commitment from local officials meant that the future of the district was in jeopardy. Every election was full of promises by local politicians, yet every year the budget deficit became larger. The new gambling boats that were docked on the river to the east of the city were supposed to resolve the mounting deficit, but 3 years later the school district has yet to see much of the money that it was promised.

Mr. Gaskins's classroom is a pretty bland affair, far from a fountain of intellectual and emotional stimulation. The old gray walls have paint flaking off. The only color comes from a bulletin board that contains faded pictures of famous scientists. In the room, all 32 chairs are lined neatly in rows, with just barely enough room for even an adult to squeeze by. Mr. Gaskins's teaching is driven by the need to cover a specific amount of content material each week in order to cover the full sequence of annual achievement test items. Like other teachers, he has complained about the inordinate emphasis on achievement testing and how this emphasis has taken away teacher enthusiasm and thrown cold water on the magic moments when teachers finally make the connection with students—"the spark of learning," as he liked to call it.

Stanley, despite being labeled behavior disordered (BD), was basically indistinguishable from the other students in the class; he was bored with the class and sick of school. Most of the students did not read the textbook or complete the countless worksheets that Mr. Gaskins required of his students. Mr. Gaskins called the students "lazy" and often blamed their lack of effort on their "deprived environment" rather than on his own teaching or curriculum.

For Stanley, his BD label was just that—a label. He had been identified as BD 3 years ago following a solid 6 weeks of disruptive behavior. Despite his achievement in his classes, his excellent social skills, and his clean disciplinary record since that time, he remains categorized as BD. Stanley lives at home with his mother and older brother, Sharnel. Their parents have been divorced for 5 years, and often both children have expressed to their mother how difficult it is not to see their father. The divorce came about because of their father's continuous physical abuse of their mother. Having witnessed the beatings, both boys realize that it is probably better that they don't see their father for a while. Because Stanley's mother works the night shift at a local bar, the boys are on their own in the evenings. They often have to prepare for school on their own in the morning because their mother is usually sleeping. On this particular day, Stanley was sleepy because he was up all night watching TV and would have missed school if not for his brother.

CRYING AND MARCHING

✎ THE INCIDENT

Mr. Craig, a first-year teacher at Valley Trails Elementary School, looked briefly at little Zach Will and then nervously scanned the busy cafeteria. He quickly realized that there were no other teachers in this enormous room full of noisy children. He alone would have to deal with Zach, the fourth-grade boy who seemed to cry for at least 30 minutes every day. Zach was sitting alone at the end of a cafeteria bench, his fingers gently rolling a cold Tater Tot back and forth against the side of his face. The other children had cleared out, backed off, giving Zach space at the first sign of tears. Face bright red, tears rolling like the Mississippi during spring thaw, he was crying softly to himself.

As Mr. Craig walked hesitantly across the cafeteria toward Zach, he hardly noticed the rumbling din of 200 young children socializing over cheeseburgers and green Jell-O. His mind filled with images from his own childhood. He recalled the day he went to see his father for the first time. He was 10 years old. His mother drove him up to the front gate of the property. He walked up and sat on the front porch with this strange and enormous man. They talked for 15 minutes, the distance between them growing more acute and glaring with each awkward word. Finally, little Billy Craig jumped off the porch and ran to the car where his mother waited. He cried all the way home, his head resting in her lap as she drove.

Suddenly, Mr. Craig recalled the staff meeting in which his principal, Ms. Debaliviere, outlined the plan for dealing with Zach Will's frequent episodes of crying.

"That crying behavior is pure manipulation," Ms. Debaliviere had explained. "He wants attention and has to learn not to seek it in a negative way. When he exhibits the crying behavior, wherever that may be, simply and firmly march him down to my office."

Looking up, Mr. Craig realized that he had arrived. He had walked across the cafeteria and was now standing 2 feet from 9-year-old Zach. Zach's tears were still flowing.

"Let's go, Zach," Mr. Craig heard himself saying in a surprisingly sharp tone. "You know the drill. Down to the office. Let's march." Zach walked peaceably with the teacher to the office, tears running fully with every step. At the boy's side marched Mr. Craig. His powerful sense of discomfort about punishing a boy for crying raged silently as he simply did his professional duty.

BACKGROUND INFORMATION

Much vital insight into this situation may be gleaned from a glimpse into the vocalized words and silent thoughts of the various professionals who attended the staff meeting concerning Zach. At that meeting, held a week before this incident, Ms. Debaliviere detailed the intervention plan calling for teachers to "march" this crying youngster to the office.

When Ms. Debaliviere holds a staff meeting, she directs the discussion with a no-nonsense attitude and one eye on her wristwatch. She hands out an agenda of discussion items to the teachers. Next to each item is an incremental time allotment, typically between 2 and 5 minutes per topic. Principal Debaliviere tends to talk about each item for most of the time allotment. When she opens up an item for discussion, the teachers are generally silent. They simply await her decision on the matter.

Ms. Normandy, Zach's third-grade teacher, was surprised to see *Zach Will's crying* listed as the third agenda item for that October 19 staff meeting. After quickly moving through two minor issues concerning bus duty and the upcoming visit by the regional assistant superintendent, Ms. Debaliviere addressed item 3, a 2-minute item.

"Agenda item number 3, a disciplinary item. Zachary Will of Ms. Normandy's class has had 10 extended crying jags over the course of 3 weeks. These episodes have been lasting over 30 minutes. Three have occurred in Ms. Normandy's classroom, five in the cafeteria, one in the front hallway, one in Mr. Edelson's music class. I've seen this sort of thing before, one student drawing the attention of the teacher in a negative way and thereby disrupting the learning process for others. Some of you may recall a little girl in Ms. Beezeley's room a few years back. Eunice, who was that girl?"

"Her name was Wendy Watkins," replied Eunice Beezeley, a veteran teacher. "She cried every day for a week, if I recall correctly."

"Yes, Eunice, that's the one," Principal Debaliviere continued. "Wendy Watkins would go on for an hour. We instituted a plan whereby Ms. Beezeley sent Wendy to the office at the first sign of a tear. It was crucial not to wait on this behavior. Ms. Beezeley intervened quickly, brought the child to my office, and I set her in a time-out chair in the corner behind the large filing cabinet. The child only needed to be sent to me twice and the problem was solved."

As Ms. Debaliviere recalled this experience from the past and then briefly detailed the plan for all teachers to implement the same intervention with Zach Will, the teachers of Valley Trails Elementary School listened silently. Behind their silence stirred much information and insight concerning this situation. The thoughts of Ms. Beezeley, Ms. Ellis, and Mr. Craig provide us with much information about this problem of Zach's crying.

Ms. Beezeley wondered why little Zach was crying. She recalled that many months after the intervention that effectively halted Wendy Watkins's crying bouts, she had bumped into Wendy's mother at the supermarket. Wendy's mother thanked Ms. Beezeley for teaching Wendy to truly love reading. As Eunice Beezeley felt the sweet glow of satisfaction, Ms. Watkins went on to explain how reading had been a source of tremendous solace to Wendy after the death of her grandfather. Ms. Beezeley recalled that she had asked tear-flushed Wendy over and over, "What's wrong? Why are you crying?" But Wendy had never explained. She just blubbered on and on. Ms. Beezeley wished she had known about Wendy's grandfather's death much earlier.

Ms. Ellis, the school guidance counselor, recalled that she had almost met with Zach's mother this past spring. There had been a class field trip to the aquarium, and Zach had forgotten to return his permission slip. Ms. Ellis had called simply to ask Zach's mother if her boy could go on the trip. Little Zach sat in the beanbag chair across from the guidance counselor, eyes downcast at the thought of not going on the trip. He hadn't cried at all, Ms. Ellis recalled. Zach's mother approved the field trip and asked to meet with Ms. Ellis to discuss some difficulties she was having with Zach at home. Apparently, Zach's father had moved out, and a new boyfriend had moved in, stirring some issues and misbehavior on Zach's part. From the anxious tone in the mother's voice, Ms. Ellis interpreted that there was much more to the story than a boy having trouble adjusting to a new father figure. Ms. Ellis recalled setting up a meeting to discuss the problem, but Zach's mother hadn't shown up. When she subsequently didn't return three of Ms. Ellis's phone calls, the counselor had allowed the issue to drop.

Mr. Craig, an eager new teacher, spent the meeting diligently recording Principal Debaliviere's directions in his notebook. As the principal described the problem of Zach Will's crying, Mr. Craig pictured himself sitting down next to the lad on the floor, consoling the evidently sad youngster. This was the type of caring that Mr. Craig had hoped to bring to children by becoming a teacher. Then he noticed that his principal spoke about problems and solutions with an incredible degree of self-assurance. She seemed to know immediately exactly what to do in each situation. Her voice and demeanor were filled with the kind of confidence that he knew he lacked. He thought about his professional struggle to become more of a firm authority with the children. His first month of teaching had been a nightmare. He offered continuous kindness and his class of fifth graders walked all over him. Ms. Debaliviere and the other teachers began coaching him to "get tough" and "lay down the law." Since then, he has been trying to strike some sort of balance between kindness and authority, caring and power. Before he could fully consider this dilemma, Mr. Craig's attention was broken by the principal's voice.

"Agenda item number 4, the implementation of a new science curriculum."

CASE **6**

DEMOLITION DAN

 THE INCIDENT

"Boom! Boom!" shouted Danny as he jumped up and down. His small frame quivered with excitement. At his feet lay a pile of blocks that Caitlin had previously stacked neatly in the shape of a house. When Caitlin looked up from the water fountain, she let out a loud scream. Meanwhile Danny just kept repeating "Boom, boom, boom" as he ran to Cynthia's play area.

Using her arms as a shield to protect her block building, little Cynthia shouted at him, "No, Danny! No! No!" It was too late; her building came crashing to the ground. Danny stood over it jumping up and down, screaming "Boom! Boom!" By the time Eileen Hattson had grabbed Danny's arm, he was already on his way to another play site, with the possibility of destroying another child's block building.

"Danny, you do not destroy other kids' blocks," Eileen told the boy as she bent down to look at him at eye level. But Danny, uninterested in listening to another lecture about "appropriate" behavior, looked away and continued jumping up and down. "Look at me! Look at me!" Eileen insisted. She then took him by the hand, walked over to Caitlin's pile of blocks, and requested that Danny help her build a new house. "Think about what you did and how sad you made Caitlin feel," lectured Eileen. "You need to learn not to destroy other children's work," she reiterated as she sat him on her lap in front of the blocks.

 BACKGROUND INFORMATION

Immediately prior to this incident, Danny became angry on the playground. Coming in from recess, Danny was still quite angry about the incident that occurred outside. On the playground, Danny was teased by two older children who thought his little body and large head looked odd. They began calling him names, and he responded by kicking their toys. He was still kicking when Eileen grabbed him by the arm and helped him inside the school. Once inside, Eileen got the children involved in activities on small carpet squares. Each child was expected to play on a carpet square for only 10 minutes before he or she moved on to the next activity. After another 10 minutes, like clockwork, each child moved to another carpet square.

Currently, Danny is enrolled in Ms. Hattson's preschool class, a program affiliated with Ocean Mist University. The Ocean Mist Preschool is run by Dorothy Perkins, a graduate of Ocean Mist, who utilizes a constructivist approach to classroom management. For Danny this means that the solutions to his behavioral problems occur by helping him to gain a more active understanding of his actions and how those actions affect others. Ms. Perkins believes that only through a more active self-understanding of a child's actions can each child understand the social and moral value of those actions and be more willing to possibly change his or her behavior. For most children, this constructivist approach has led to a successful resolution of their inappropriate behaviors; for others, many of their actions continue to cause social unrest among their classmates.

Although Danny has been labeled developmentally delayed in the areas of social competence and language skills, he has managed to fit in well with his classmates—some of whom have disabilities. The 12 students in the class, as a group, have functioned well in their cooperative learning environment. Over the past 3 months, Eileen has taught the students to develop a buddy system for both play and learning. Students are teamed in duos and taught to help and look out for the well-being of their buddies. Buddies are exchanged on a periodic basis to give children experiences playing and learning with different peers. Now in her second year of teaching, Eileen has enjoyed working with the variety of students who come from different and varied cultures. On the whole, she has done well at teaching her students appropriate educational and social skills, but Danny continually gives her problems with his "destructive" nature.

Nicknamed "Demolition Dan" by his teacher, Danny often gets into confrontations with other students and frequently destroys their projects (i.e., artwork, toys, and worksheets). Danny loves to tear paper. Eileen has learned that she needs to keep all paper products out of Danny's sight. On one recent occasion, when she left Danny alone in the room for a few minutes, she returned to confetti-like pieces of her newspaper spread out on the floor. After making Danny clean up the mess, she decided to never again leave him unattended. This pattern of destroying objects has occurred at other times as well. For example, a few days ago, Danny managed to sneak Anthony's show-and-tell project, a tape recorder, from his desk and, within 30 seconds, had it smashed in pieces on the ground.

Danny currently lives with his foster parents, Lucy and Hank Contor, and six other foster children. Lucy and Hank have had similar problems with Danny at home. For instance, Hank recently told Eileen that when Danny wanted a milkshake, he crawled up on the counter, grabbed the blender, and threw it on the floor. In the past, Hank had used the blender to make homemade milkshakes for the kids. It is now broken, and a gate at the entrance to their kitchen keeps Danny from possibly damaging the other kitchen appliances. In addition to his indoor escapades, Danny has also wreaked a fair amount of havoc outside the Contor household. A few weeks ago when Danny was playing outside, he somehow crawled under the fence to the garden. When Lucy noticed that he was missing, she called Hank and a search of the family property ensued. After 10 minutes, Lucy found Danny hidden behind the tomato plants, tearing out the plants by their roots.

In teacher-parent conferences, both Eileen and Lucy agree that Danny needs to work on his destructiveness and his language problems. For a 3-year-old, Danny communicates with a limited number of vocabulary words. Often Danny is able to make his requests known through grunts or a small repertoire of words and hand gestures. His language skills are believed to be delayed for reasons both neurological and social. It seems that his neurological development is slow in language areas. Also, it is possible that his foster family supports his lack of language use. His six siblings are always around to assist Danny and eagerly get him whatever he wants, thereby reducing his need to communicate with words. Usually, Danny has appropriate interactions with his siblings until his destructive actions cause problems. Realizing that someday Danny will be leaving, his temporary family do their best to deal with him.

CASE 7

DEPEND ON ME

THE INCIDENT

A small squabble was brewing between two 3-year-olds in the bright yellow sandbox area in the corner of the classroom. As Sandy Brown attempted to walk across her classroom to deal with the problem, her right leg dragged as if it were attached to a large sack of flour. She smiled at her friend Felix Gassoway, a university classmate and observer in her class. She pointed at her dragging leg and mouthed the word *Jason*. Felix, knowing full well to whom she was referring, twisted his head sideways and furrowed his brow, as if to say, "Jason? What Jason? I don't see any Jason." Sandy shot Felix a mock scowl and limped as quickly as possible toward the mini-battle stewing in the sandbox. Jason hung on tight for every step.

Felix and Sandy were graduate students collaborating on an action research project for a special education course at a nearby university. One morning per week, Felix observed in Sandy's class and took extensive field notes on behavior problems. Sandy read his weekly reports and wrote back her own observations and thoughts concerning behavior problems in her classroom.

As Sandy walked past Felix, the body of a small boy clinging desperately to the teacher's leg became visible. He was losing his grip on her slacks, sliding down, and mumbling a list of preverbal demands. Finally, Sandy scooped the boy up with her hand and pulled him up to the relative safety of her hip. Felix watched Sandy tote this youngster around as she taught the other children for the next half hour, then he jotted this down in his observational field notes: "The boy must be 4 years old. He is much too large to be carried around like an infant. Yet he repeatedly demands that Ms. Brown carry him. Very dependent. Can this dependency be decreased? Is Ms. Brown only nurturing this dependency by holding him so much? And how does this affect the other children? Last question: Why is the paraprofessional sitting at her desk while Ms. Brown is running from needy child to needy child?"

BACKGROUND INFORMATION

Sandy Brown is a second-year teacher at the Alliance Preschool, a program that fully includes youngsters with disabilities or developmental delays with their typical age peers. Her classroom paraprofessional is Ella Williamson, a 14-year veteran of various special education classrooms throughout the district. This is her fifth year in the inclusive preschool program.

Jason is a 4-year-old boy who was adopted 2 years ago from an orphanage in Romania. His adoptive parents saw a program on television showing the atrocious, overcrowded conditions in many Romanian orphanages and decided to save one child from that terrible fate. Jason undoubtedly bears the emotional scars of an infancy spent in an institution lacking clean water, healthy food, and adequate loving contact with adults. He has additional developmental delays that may be unrelated to the poor care he received as a baby. His speech is loud but very diffi-cult to understand. He speaks a repertoire of about 20 words. His listening compre-hension is far more advanced, close to that of age peers. Additionally, he seems to have a neurological impairment that cannot yet be clearly diagnosed. His gross motor functioning is similar to age peers, but his fine motor skills are significantly delayed. His hands and arms are weak and poorly coordinated. He has tremendous difficulty holding a crayon or scooping up sand with a spoon. At times, Jason has displayed behaviors typical of autism; specifically, Jason has held his hands up between his eyes and the overhead lights, fixating visually on the play of light across the motion of his fingers. Sometimes he has sat off by himself, rocking his body and repeating a single word or phrase for 15 to 20 minutes.

Socially, Jason tends to have little interest in his peers. He is able to play or learn in a small group of children, but his attention inevitably zeroes in on an adult. Generally, with an occasional exception when Ella will hold Jason at her desk, Jason has sought out Sandy's affection. Sandy has been baffled about what to do. She finds herself literally carrying Jason around for half of her time. She has tried setting him down and directing him to play with a favorite toy or work on an activity, but this has frequently brought on a crying bout or a spell of body rocking and verbal rumi-nation. With Ella's encouragement ("You must break him of this nonsense"), Sandy once allowed Jason to cry for over 40 minutes before she finally returned to scoop him up and dry his eyes. He just doesn't seem able to get along without her.

Sandy asked her university classmate Felix to observe closely and try to offer some solutions for handling Jason. By reading Felix's notes, Sandy has learned that she carries Jason around much more than she realized. It is not uncommon that Sandy organizes and leads the other children in a group activity such as singing a song while holding Jason on her hip. Like a habitual smoker who notices the ciga-rette in her mouth but does not recall lighting one up, Sandy carries Jason around without even noticing what she is doing.

Although Sandy originally directed Felix to concentrate his observations on her difficulties with Jason, Felix's notes soon shifted to something he found equally interesting—that is, the way that Ella remained at her desk at the front of the class-room for hours at a time, interacting very little with the children. In reading Felix's notes, Sandy soon realized that she was doing 80% to 90% of the direct work with the children while Ella remained very distant and uninvolved. If a child specifically went to Ella, she would respond and play with the child. But Ella rarely initiated interaction with the youngsters. Sandy admitted to Felix that as a young teacher she felt as if she had entered a classroom owned by Ella. Although she is officially

Ella's supervisor, she has felt little authority in critiquing and correcting her older colleague's work habits.

By the end of the semester, Felix had begun to write small interpretations and questions that brought together the two problems (i.e., Jason's dependency and Ella's lack of involvement with the students). He noted that some of the other children seemed to resent Jason for monopolizing their teacher's affections. At times, he connected the angry or sad moods of certain youngsters to their inability to gain access to their teacher's love and attention. Felix wondered if this situation couldn't be alleviated by the active participation of one other adult, namely Ella. How would the active involvement of that one adult help to satisfy the needs for nurturing and affection that were so obvious in Jason and quite evident in the other children?

After talking to Felix about Ella's lack of involvement with the students, Sandy decided to seek the advice of the director of the Alliance Preschool, Dr. Amy Chu. Dr. Chu had been a professor of child development at Eastern State University before she decided to leave academic work to found Alliance, an experimental preschool program in a major city. The program consists of a staff of four certified teachers and four teacher aides, supplemented by a number of parent volunteers. A total of 55 youngsters between the ages of 3 and 5 are served.

The Alliance Preschool, now 5 years old, is located in an old plastics factory building within easy walking distance from the low-income housing apartments where over a thousand families live. Soon after the doors opened that first August, the professionals found themselves working side by side with a small but dedicated group of parent volunteers from the neighborhood. Most of the volunteers are mothers in their late teens who left high school to have children. Those volunteers founded a small GED study program on the Alliance site in the evenings. Sandy has taught some of the classes designed to help the parents earn their GEDs and move on to community college or vocational programs.

Many local educators, Sandy included, consider Dr. Chu to be something of a visionary in the field of early childhood education. Dr. Chu openly rejects the common language-based approach utilized in many preschools that serve urban children of color. She believes adamantly that these predominantly African-American and Hispanic children do not require a constant message that their spoken dialect is "wrong" and in need of correction. In her oft-repeated words: "How could a child who is told daily that her words are wrong in comparison with an abstraction called 'standard English' develop any self-esteem?" Instead, Dr. Chu has developed an exploratory arts-based program in which the youngsters are given opportunities to produce aesthetic and cultural symbols such as drawings, paintings, and clay figures.

The teachers of Alliance share Dr. Chu's vision, but they also find their director to be a difficult person to approach with everyday problems. In some ways, Dr. Chu tends to be a hands-off administrator. She handles the budget, makes a number of high-profile speaking engagements promoting the school and raising funds throughout the state, and works closely with her teachers on the development of the arts-based curriculum. When it comes to mundane matters involving conflicts between adults, Dr. Chu seems either not to care or simply not to know what to do.

With a fair amount of hesitancy, Sandy approached her supervisor with her issue regarding Ella Williamson. She explained Felix's observations and her desire that Ella get out from behind her desk and be active with the children. Dr. Chu listened carefully and assured Sandy that she would talk to Ella about this issue without letting on that Sandy had complained. As she walked out of the director's office, Sandy felt relieved and hopeful.

For the next 3 weeks, Sandy saw a marked improvement in Ella's work. She played with the children and even toted Jason for up to a half hour at a time. It even seemed that she might be able to teach Jason a little independence. She would carry him for a while, then set him down and play with him, gradually creating some distance between herself and this very dependent toddler. After the 3 good weeks, however, Sandy noticed Ella slipping back into her old habits, sitting behind her desk instead of participating among the students.

C A S E **8**

CRASHING PLANES AND TRANQUIL DREAMS

THE INCIDENT

As nap time approached, Sandy Werton knew it was going to be another rough day because Richard had arrived at school more active than ever. "That boy has more energy than I ever had at his age," Sandy commented to Jill Bosco, the aide in the class. Sandy looked at her watch and announced to her class, "Well, it's 12 o'clock. Nap time." With her comment, the six students in her class let out a chorus of moans. At the time, most students were busy playing with their toys, except for Richard, who was running around the room pretending to be an airplane. Within a few minutes, the students were nestled down on their mats with small white blankets covering them, except for Richard, who was practicing "emergency landing" procedures, accompanied by screeching noises to simulate the twisting metal of a plane crash.

"Richard, this is the second time I've had to tell you to get over here to lie down." Sandy spoke in a low but firm voice. Richard, oblivious to anything but the plane wreck, continued to play. Sandy, moving closer to him, again spoke. "Richard, get yourself over here and lie down."

This time Richard looked up and, realizing that he was the only one not lying down, cried out, "I don't wanna nap now. I no tired now." To these responses, Sandy lifted him up and carried his small but wiry body over to his mat.

"Look, Richard, you need to sleep. Every day we go over this. It is time for your nap. Now, let's go. Get to sleep!" explained Sandy in a hushed voice. She set him down gently on his mat. As soon as Sandy walked away from Richard, he got up, began making airplane noises, and ran toward his toy plane sitting on the shelf. For Sandy, this battle with Richard was an almost daily occurrence.

BACKGROUND INFORMATION

Richard finally fell asleep. It took Sandy 20 minutes to get him settled and quiet. After many threats, yelling, and tears (Richard's), he finally closed his eyes. Although the quiet room was a respite for Sandy, it did not last long. Ten minutes later, Richard was awake, giggling and laughing. Sandy called over to him to be quiet, but she knew that he would be awake for the rest of the school day. Jill, back from lunch, saw Richard awake and ran over to quiet him down. After a few fruit-less minutes, she directed him to some toys in the box. Meanwhile, Sandy was busy writing notes to send home. Again, Sandy had to report that Richard did not sleep very long and that there was an incident in the bathroom in which Richard had thrown a cup of water on another student. As Sandy wrote the note for Richard's parents, she again contemplated how best to handle Richard. She has tried to get him to nap by taking away his recess, taking away his snack, and threatening to call his parents, but has had no luck. The director of the program has suggested that she use stickers or candy to reinforce his behavior on those days when he follows the rules, but Sandy felt that this would not be fair to the rest of the class.

Richard, now 4 years old, has been in the YMCA's full-day preschool program for the past 2 years. Richard gets along fairly well with other students, although his parents and teachers often comment about his "hyper" behavior. They suspect that he might have an attention deficit disorder, but he has yet to be formally diagnosed. Aside from his "hyper" behavior, impulsiveness, and an occasional battle with adults, Richard is generally thought of as a "good" kid who occasionally gets into trouble. He is bright and well liked by the other children and adults. He often surprises adults with pictures drawn for them, along with words of "I love you." His sweet smile and funny facial expressions often negate any bad news that he brings home.

Richard lives at home with two brothers, Zarell and David, aged 9 and 10. His parents, Tom and Latisha Green, realize that Richard is, at times, overly active, but they often blame his hyperactivity on excessive sweets or drinks. Tom does not spend a lot of time at home. He has a busy schedule that includes a lot of overtime work, needed to help pay the bills, and a number of commitments with the church and local Little League. When Tom does spend time with Richard, he usually ends up yelling at him or sending him to his room for getting into things that he shouldn't have gotten into (e.g., Tom's toolbox, the birdseed, or the trash). Because of Tom and Latisha's religious convictions, they spend a lot of time in church or involved in church-related activities. Church is another setting where Richard frequently gets in trouble. He is constantly out of his seat, and sometimes he inadvertently makes noises. These behaviors have embarrassed the parents on a number of occasions and resulted in Richard being taken outside to receive a spanking.

Because child care at the YMCA is expensive, Latisha often works long hours, resulting in 10- to 12-hour days at preschool (including the before- and after-school program) for Richard. Latisha regrets working long hours and often considers quitting the "rat race" for shorter days and more quality time with her children. Latisha has left work on more than one occasion to attend to her children's needs at school and home. Her busy schedule frequently keeps her from enjoying life with her kids, but the difficult reality of a two-person working family holds true for the Greens.

Zarell, Richard's older brother, has a quick temper and tends to get in fights at school. About one day per month, Latisha receives a phone call from Zarell's school—because he has gotten into another fight. Latisha tells her boss and dashes off to school to pick up Zarell. As she drives to school, she wonders how Richard is doing and contemplates how many future trips she will have to make to one of her sons' schools to resolve problems.

At home, Richard gets yelled at quite a few times during the evening because, as Latisha states, "he just doesn't listen sometimes." Latisha and Tom use yelling and "the chair" (time-out) as their forms of management, and these methods seem to work well. For example, last evening Richard did not eat all of his dinner; actually, he only ate a few bites of food. Even before finishing his meal, he asked Latisha for a candy bar. When she refused to give one to him, Richard threw himself on the floor and began kicking and crying. Latisha yelled at him to stop and threatened to put him on "the chair." Then, realizing that she doesn't spend much time with him, she gave in and handed him the candy bar. This pattern of behavior and response is common for the two; that is, he yells, she threatens, and then she gives in. By the time Tom arrives home, typically around 8 o'clock, any problems that have arisen are resolved. Usually, Richard is asleep in his bed, and the other two boys are wrestling on the floor while the TV plays in the background.

CASE 9

FIFTEEN SECONDS OF FAME

THE INCIDENT

As Henry Hennison looked down the hallway, his eyes lit up in amazement. Blowing up and down on the hallway walls were pieces of paper that represented each child's artwork, homework, or special project. All day long as students walked down the center of the hallway, papers taped to the walls on both sides blew at them in every direction. It was actually a stimulating tactile experience as the sides of their bodies were gently touched by paper or paper products. As in many schools, the papers or projects from every classroom that hung outside each room were chosen to showcase each child's best work. On this particular hot, windy day, each classroom had the windows and doors open, creating a "wind tunnel" effect in the hall. The cool breeze felt good on the tired brows of the countless children who made trips to the bathroom located at the far end of the hall.

With the hall now empty, Henry suddenly had an enlightened idea. Backing up to the outside doors, Henry announced his ambitious intentions with the words, "Ready, set, go!" He then took off at full speed down the hallway with his arms stretched wide, grabbing as many papers off the walls as he could. In his tracks lay the remains of his destructive drag race: ripped papers spread all over the hallway floor. When he neared the end of the hallway, a pair of large hands reached out from nowhere to grab him by the shirt collar and reel him in from his pillaging run. The hands belonged to none other than Mr. George Dillard, the school's principal. Looking down the messy hallway, Mr. Dillard's lower jaw dropped and his voice trembled with anger. "What are you doing?" hollered Mr. Dillard. Before Henry could answer, Mr. Dillard shouted again, "What in the world have you done?" Realizing that his 15-second fantasy drag race had landed him in the hands of an angry principal, Henry began to cry uncontrollably. With tears rolling down his small face, he realized that his impulsiveness had again gotten him in trouble. Meanwhile, down the hall, curious students poked their heads out the doors to see what had happened.

BACKGROUND INFORMATION

Some temptations in life are just too good to pass by. Unfortunately, for Henry many temptations in life are too good to pass by. Although he is only 7, Henry's impulsiveness has gotten him into more predicaments than most children twice his age. "Immature," "out of control," and "wild" are the words that he has heard over and over again to describe him and his behavior. Yesterday, his teacher scolded him for banging on the computer keyboard as the other children were typing in information. Two days ago, he engaged the car engine from park to drive when his mother, Yolanda, stepped out of the vehicle to put a package in the trunk. Jerking forward, the car rolled 10 yards and plowed into the garage door. Last Saturday, he almost electrocuted himself after he stuck a fork into the videotape player when his *Toy Story* videotape wouldn't eject. Last week, Henry pushed his classmate, Lucy, down the steps when she suddenly stopped in front of him. Henry claimed it was an accident.

Henry has had many such "accidents" in his life. Yolanda often remarks that she "could write a book" about Henry's trials and tribulations. Almost daily Yolanda hears from his teacher, a neighbor, or other children about Henry's latest destructive or dangerous acts. For her, no news is the best news. Yolanda feels that Henry is a "good-hearted" child who does not really mean to harm other people or break things. Consequently, when Henry does get into trouble, Yolanda calmly talks to him about the incident, tells him to be "more careful next time," and then sends him back to whatever he was doing. It is only on rare occasions that Yolanda sends Henry to his room. Yolanda also feels that Henry sometimes "acts up" because he is having trouble dealing with her separation from his father, Harry.

After Henry's latest incident, the hallway race, Mr. Dillard sent him to see the school counselor, Ms. Carrie Anthan. Ms. Anthan has seen Henry on a weekly to twice weekly basis. Her file on Henry described a troubled child who often seeks attention through inappropriate actions. In personal counseling sessions with her, Henry has told Ms. Anthan of his racing thoughts and lack of control in turning thoughts into actions. She feels that Henry is actually depressed and often acts out in reaction to his sad thoughts. She has tried a number of interventions with him, including substituting positive for negative thoughts and counting to 10 before reacting to irrational thoughts, a lot of "heavy stuff" for a 7-year-old. In reaction to some of her more complex suggestions, Henry once blurted out, "I'm only seven years old." Although Ms. Anthan and Yolanda have spoken about Henry's behavior and possible remedies, Yolanda often dismisses her suggestions as "psychological mumbo jumbo" and often dismisses Henry's actions as those of a typical 7-year-old.

Henry's father, whom the lad sees on weekends, also has to deal with many of the same inappropriate actions. The difference is that Harry deals differently with little Henry's behavior. Harry's approach to dealing with Henry involves slapping him on the buttocks. This method of discipline usually works out well for Harry and in the short run, Henry behaves. Henry respects and, at times, fears his father. Henry has talked to Yolanda about his fear of his father and his reluctance to visit him. However, when Yolanda spoke to Harry about Henry's fears, Harry dismissed it as the foolish talk of a child and even told Yolanda that she should try being stern with Henry to help him control his behavior. Despite Henry's improved behavior after a spanking, it doesn't take him long before he is again in trouble with his father.

CASE 10

WHEN FEAR RULES THE LAND

THE INCIDENT

While the shrieks of joy were heard from children playing games on the front playground, behind the school a very different story was unfolding. Off in a quiet area behind a row of thick shrubs came a "thump" followed by the muted sounds of a young child crying. It was Maryjo Hanley beating up a smaller child who had challenged her authority. "Next time I want to copy your homework you better let me or else you'll get more of this," whispered Maryjo into the ear of her latest victim, Fran Klenck. Maryjo and her two sidekicks, Leeanne and Shirley, released Fran from their grip.

Fran, with an ache in her stomach and tears streaming down her cheeks, ran to a vacant corner of the playground and hid her face in shame. Her mind wandered back to last week. On Monday, she had volunteered her spelling homework for Maryjo to copy. The surprised bully accepted the gift with a confused grin. All week Fran had made an extreme effort to befriend Maryjo. Due to her efforts, the daily intimidation sessions miraculously subsided. It had been the first time during the school year that Fran wasn't afraid to go to school.

This week, Fran had second thoughts about the ethics of handing over her completed homework to Maryjo. She worked so hard to get a good grade, and Maryjo did nothing at all. It just didn't seem fair. She didn't give her homework to Maryjo for one day, and this was her payment, a nasty drubbing in the bushes.

BACKGROUND INFORMATION

Fran's mother, Wella, has suspected for some time that something is wrong. It seems that almost every morning Fran complains about a different minor illness—nausea, headaches, lightheadedness. When Wella confronts Fran about her illnesses, Fran cries and says that she wants to stay home from school because she doesn't feel very good.

"If I just stay home today, I'll feel better," Fran insists in a tearful, babyish tone.

If Wella probes further, Fran's crying increases until she begins coughing and choking with tears. If Wella suggests that she call the school, Fran becomes very defensive, insisting that nothing is wrong in school. She just feels sick. Without Fran's knowledge, on one occasion Wella has called the school and spoken to her teacher, Nora Johanson. Ms. Johanson told Wella that she had not noticed anything different in Fran's behavior, although she did admit that with 30 kids, it was difficult to keep an eye on each of them.

Maryjo carefully selected her victims and chose only those who would submit to her torment and at the same time remain quiet. With Fran, she found the perfect target. Fran was one of the smartest and one of the shyest students in the class. She would easily submit to Maryjo, partly because Fran feared Maryjo and her gang and partly because Fran wanted to be friends with any student in the class. New to the area, Fran badly wanted friends. At her old school, Fran had some friends, but only one or two of them could be considered true friends. For Fran her newest friendship (or manipulative partnership) was a little like having a pal in the Mafia in that such friendships come with a price tag attached.

Maryjo and her partners rule with fear. Now in the sixth grade, Maryjo can finally effectively rule the playground and other low-structure school settings without older children challenging her authority. Maryjo has sought after the control and the power that comes with her strength, size (she was the tallest sixth-grade student in her class), and fierce demeanor.

In Maryjo's family, physical and verbal abuse are everyday experiences. Her stepfather, Jack Hanley, is the source of most of the abuse in their household. Through Jack's beatings, Maryjo quickly learned that hitting and intimidation are two effective and frightening methods for a powerful person to use to get what he or she wants. Mary Hanley, Maryjo's mother, puts up with the abuse because she is too afraid of her husband to take any meaningful action. Also, she is too embarrassed to admit the abuse and seek help from family, friends, or professionals. Mary often rationalizes Jack's violent actions as warranted because she did something wrong or because Maryjo was bugging her father. Jack doesn't need to be drunk to hit Mary or Maryjo, but the frequency of the beatings increases when he is intoxicated. When Jack isn't at work at the local glass factory, he can usually be found at the VFW bar. On a number of occasions, Jack and Mary have received complaints from neighbors about Maryjo's bullying behavior, but they dismiss it as typical childhood behavior.

Ms. Johanson has had a difficult time monitoring the behavior of her 30 students. It took her 2 full months until she was able to learn all of their names. Now in her third year, Ms. Johanson has the reputation of being a "spacey" teacher. Often underprepared and wishy-washy when handling on-the-spot decisions, she has become the butt of jokes among the school's faculty.

Ms. Johanson has spent so much time this year dealing with behavioral problems that she has fallen drastically behind in the curriculum—compared with the other sixth-grade classes. In order to make up some of her lost time, she has sent home larger amounts of homework than she normally would, resulting in a number of parent complaints. Her current method of dealing with behavior problems is to send the culprit into the hall for 5 minutes. Once in the hallway, Ms. Johanson usually scolds the offender and threatens to call his or her parents. If the misbehavior is very serious, she sends the child to the principal's office. Her classroom is noisy and chaotic, often a stressful place to be. When the principal observes Ms. Johanson for her quarterly evaluation, he is overwhelmed by the beehive of motion and sound. He leaves the room with a headache and a list of critical comments on the evaluation form. With her job on the line, Ms. Johanson has already considered looking for other jobs.

CASE **11**

GAMEY SCIENCE

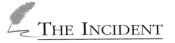 THE INCIDENT

"Books open. Notebooks out. Eyes on me!" bellows Mr. Entenmann. As he calls his eighth-grade science class to order, this veteran teacher attempts to hide his anxieties beneath the fullness of his strong voice. He knows that his last-period class has become increasingly unsettled and unruly in the past few weeks. Officially speaking, they have not been breaking classroom or school rules; the disruptive behavior has been playful, sarcastic, subtle, and smart. The students have attempted to lure or coax Mr. Entenmann into a jousting match, a tense verbal game in which the victor controls the classroom. The result is that Mr. Entenmann has often looked silly and the day's lecture has been sidetracked, delayed, and even lost. As Mr. Entenmann calls the class to order, he is mentally prepared to ward off any such silliness.

Before Mr. Entenmann can begin his lecture, Billy calls out from the front row. "Mr. Entenmann, I've been thinking a lot about these bases and acids and I have an important question."

"Yes," replies Mr. Entenmann hesitantly, wondering whether to encourage student interest or stop the tomfoolery before it gets started.

Billy continues. "So I'm thinking about these acids and bases flowing all over the world and I want to know—" Billy pauses here, leans back in his chair with a slight grin, and looks around to see that most of the students are watching and listening. "I want to know why the whole world isn't just rotting and deteriorating and getting eaten up by all these acids. Would you please explain that?"

Mr. Entenmann bristles slightly, his neck stiffening. He doesn't want to answer because he doubts the seriousness of the question, but he knows, too, that Billy is a top student with a good reputation. "Billy, we covered that last week. Do you have your notes from the two lectures when we covered the properties of acids?"

"Sure. I take good notes," replies Billy.

As he digs into his backpack and pulls out his notebook, Hector calls out from the back of the class. "Mr. Entenmann, I don't have that in my notes," he says as he props his chair back on two legs and smiles.

"Me either," chips in Hector's buddy Felix. His voice then trails off. He lowers his head and mumbles jokingly, so that only the back half of the class can hear, "My notes don't say anything about taking acid." The back two rows of students laugh.

"Okay. Okay. Quiet down," Mr. Entenmann demands. "I'm not covering that material again. If you don't get it the first time, you'll have to borrow the notes from someone else. Or read it in the text. The section on bases and acids begins on page 147."

"Mr. Entenmann?" queries Billy softly from the front row.

"What, Billy? We need to get started on today's material."

"I found the text's coverage of bases and acids to be somewhat spotty. Can you recommend an outside source for those of us who want to read further on the topic?" Billy smiles quasi-earnestly and turns to his friend Tony for support. Tony wrinkles his brow, nods repeatedly, and looks up at the teacher with a face of exaggerated interest.

"Quiet! No more questions!" Mr. Entenmann shouts. He has lost his patience. The tone of Billy's question sounds sincere, but it seems to be sarcastic and mocking at the same time. A hand flies up in the back of the room. It is Felix. "Felix, put your hand down," snaps Mr. Entenmann. "Keep your mouths shut, take out your notebooks, and listen. It's my turn to talk." Felix groans and drops his hand.

"But teacher," Hector spouts up, shooting a glance over to Billy, "I'm concerned that the text's coverage of this content is somewhat spotty." The class erupts in laughter.

BACKGROUND INFORMATION

In recent days, Mr. Entenmann has felt as if he has been forced to engage in a daily wrestling match with this class. He has had particular difficulty with two pairs of boys, one seated in the front and one seated in the back. The two pairs are a sharp contrast in style, reputation, and academic standing. While he has struggled with these particular two pairs, Mr. Entenmann must admit that most of the class has joined in the games as supportive participants.

Tony and Billy sit in the front of the class. These boys are members of an informal group called the Oxs, in the hallway lingo of Spring Hill Middle School. The Oxs wear button-down, oxford cloth shirts with a polo player insignia on the breast. They are neat, polite, and well spoken. They come to class fully prepared. They demonstrate a strong interest in the subject matter. Mr. Entenmann views Tony and Billy as obviously able and talented students. He taught Billy's older sister Kendra, who went on to be valedictorian of her high school class and is now attending West Point. The boys' grades on tests and quizzes place them at the top of the class. Despite their participation in the antics detailed above, Mr. Entenmann tends to see them as basically good kids.

The back row pair are another story. Mr. Entenmann is convinced that Felix and Hector could be average students if they only tried. He is frustrated because they don't apply themselves in his class. Both boys are first-generation Mexican immigrants to this country. They wear their dark hair down to their shoulders and often let it fall over their faces, as if they are hiding from their teacher and his lecture. When Felix rolls up the sleeves of his T-shirt, he sports a blue and red American eagle tattoo on his biceps. When Mr. Entenmann sees the tattoo, he thinks to himself that an eighth-grade boy shouldn't have a tattoo. He thinks to himself that if he were that boy's father, he'd clean him up and set him on the right track.

Mr. Entenmann teaches at Spring Hill Middle School, a large public school located on the Near North Side, one of the oldest suburbs of a medium-sized city. Historically, the Near North Side was developed by German immigrants who worked at the brick works or in the building trades at the turn of the century. As the city itself changed, the population of the school district now included students of many ethnic groups spanning the social class spectrum. A recent influx of Mexican and Vietnamese families to the affordable neighborhoods of Near North has changed the composition of the once homogeneous Near North schools.

Mr. Entenmann has found himself baffled by the styles of talk, clothing, and behavior of the new students. He tends to think that his job was easier before the cultural composition of the school changed. Other changes have complicated matters considerably. The district administration, once a sleeping giant in the background, has recently become very progressive and vocal, arranging workshops on multicultural education and constructivist teaching approaches for all schools. Supporting this move has been the batch of new teachers who received a similarly progressive education at the university. Additionally, the Parent-Teacher Association at Spring Hill Middle School has switched from holding bake sales to fund band trips to speaking out firmly in support of a multicultural curricular format.

If one were to interview Mr. Entenmann privately about these changes, one would discover that he is not so much against these developments as he is uncomfortable about them. He would say that things are changing much too fast. His students tell him that the other teachers don't lecture anymore, that he is old-fashioned. He is afraid that the district administration is "throwing the baby out with the bath water," forcing good teachers to change their tried-and-true teaching methods without recognizing the years of effective instruction these teachers have contributed.

Within his classroom, Mr. Entenmann feels awkward and uncertain. He has been encouraged by his building principal to send fewer students to the office on disciplinary matters. The principal wants to decrease the number of school suspensions by having the teachers and students work out more of their difficulties in the classroom. Mr. Entenmann feels somewhat inadequate in this task. He looks back fondly on the days when he could simply put his foot down and send a misbehaving student to the office.

HAT TRICK

THE INCIDENT

"Has anyone seen my hat?" asks Jack as he enters Tina Young's ninth-grade special education English class.

Kevin answers, "It's in your desk, L7."

Jack looks in his desk, but it's not there. Maurice and Kevin break out in laughter. Ms. Young looks up at the boys laughing in the back of the class, shakes her head, and goes back to marking off students on her roll.

Jack repeats his request. "Has anyone seen my hat?"

Kevin answers, "It's on the shelf."

Jack walks over to the shelf by the window and hops up on his toes to take a look. Nothing there. Maurice snickers.

"Kevin, stop teasing him," says Ms. Young.

"I'm not doing anything," Kevin says with a scowl. "I thought it was there."

Jack sits down and Maurice stops snickering.

Kevin whispers, "Check the hall. I think I saw it under a locker by the water fountain."

Jack walks out into the hall. The entire class laughs. Jack reenters the room with empty hands. Ms. Young directs Jack back to his desk by pointing at it with an index finger.

Kevin whispers to Jack, "Check the computer station." Jack casts a doubtful eye at Kevin, then he walks to the side of the room and looks in the area of the computer station, but his hat is not there. Kevin and Maurice snicker.

"Stop it, Kevin," Mrs. Young says in her serious tone of voice.

"I thought I saw him wear it at the computer station," responds Kevin innocently.

Kevin and Maurice stop laughing and Jack sits down. Kevin then points under the teacher's desk; the hat was there the entire time. As Jack gets up to retrieve the hat, the entire class laughs.

BACKGROUND INFORMATION

Kevin has been Jack's nemesis since junior high school, teasing or taunting him virtually nonstop since the beginning of the new school year. Ms. Young, their teacher, has complained to other teachers about this problem. Her colleagues agree that it is a serious problem, but no one knows how to deal with it, even though they are experienced special education teachers. Kevin is the son of Dr. Bobby Taplen, the district superintendent. Not surprisingly, Kevin has often received special treatment by teachers who were worried about saying anything negative about Dr. Taplen's boy. Kevin has gotten into trouble at school on a number of occasions, often for intimidating a peer or for fighting. Even when teachers have dared to take official disciplinary action against Kevin for his misbehavior, the standard punishments have not been administered. Typically, the principal will make a discreet phone call to his mother. She'll come pick him up and his parents will deal with the issue privately at home. For Kevin, this usually means a pretty mild reprimand from either his mother or father. Kevin is well aware of his father's influence in school. He has told his fellow classmates, "Teachers can't touch me because my dad's the boss."

Kevin is the only child in the Taplen family. Darlene and Bobby work very hard—both usually work overtime—in order to provide a comfortable life for Kevin. As a result of their work schedules, Kevin frequently goes unsupervised in the afternoon or early evening hours. When Kevin is at home, he spends most of his time in his room watching TV, exploring the Internet, or listening to rock music. When he is not at home, Kevin can usually be found at Maurice's house. Kevin and Maurice often talk about their evening escapades, replaying old classics and planning new hijinks, those mischievous adventures that typically involve acts of petty theft and vandalism upon their neighbors. These acts are mundane and small, such as covering Old Man Simpson's weeping willow tree with toilet paper, or much worse, such as the time they fed Valium to Mrs. Bleecher's poodle. The dog died. Nobody figured out who did it. Kevin and Maurice both felt guilty but rationalized their crime by telling themselves that it was an accident. They only meant to put the dog to sleep for a few hours.

To deal with Kevin's problems, he is receiving counseling from Dr. Henry Wallen, an adolescent psychologist. During his counseling sessions, Kevin has admitted that many of his behaviors can be controlled. He often doesn't feel like doing the right thing or living by the rules. That is so boring. Kevin can't stand to live the drab life his parents live. He wants excitement and the best kind of excitement is transgressing on forbidden territory. Through therapy, he has also admitted that he doesn't feel that his parents care about him. They are busy with their careers. Also, Kevin feels that he and his parents are utterly dissimilar. They walk the straight and narrow while he wants to find the wildest edge of the wild side. He thinks that he must have been adopted.

Dr. Wallen has discussed his concerns about Kevin with his parents. Darlene is a strong believer that the therapy is helping Kevin; however, Bobby does not like the therapist and consequently does not always follow up on Dr. Wallen's recommendations. Instead, Bobby feels that "grounding" Kevin is the best solution for most of Kevin's inappropriate behavior. In one recent incident, Bobby caught Kevin beating up a younger teenager. When he asked Kevin why he did it, Kevin replied, "He needs to learn a lesson that nobody back-talks Kevin Taplen." Bobby told him that he used poor judgment and grounded him for the weekend. Kevin's sentence was especially painful because that night was the school's big football game against

Ross High School. As Kevin ran to his room, he yelled out, "All you care about is being a big shot!" When he slammed the door behind him Bobby followed. Bobby approached the door, but he stopped and did not enter. He didn't know what to say, didn't know how to make things better. Kevin did not speak to his father that entire weekend. Even today, the two rarely speak.

Kevin's teasing of Jack is not an isolated incident. Kevin is a large, strong boy who frequently bullies other students. Kevin has been known to humiliate other students to the point that they cry.

Ms. Young is quick to point out how Kevin is proud of himself after his small bullying sessions with other children. Ms. Young, a firm believer in behavioral approaches to managing behaviors, feels that Kevin should not be reinforced by teachers for his inappropriate behavior. She believes that students want only one type of reinforcement in school: teacher attention. Because of her belief, she tries to use planned ignoring for any inappropriate behavior and uses teacher reinforcement for all appropriate behavior. In Kevin's case, she is simply befuddled that she couldn't extinguish his teasing behavior.

CASE 13

REPEATING HISTORY OR HISTORY REPEATING ITSELF

THE INCIDENT

"In 1775, what famous American warned other villagers in Lexington, Massachusetts, that the British were coming?" Jane Rutherman asked her ninth-grade history class. As she scanned the room for raised hands, she noticed that Felicia, once again, had her head down on her desk and appeared to be sleeping. "Jill what is the answer?" Ms. Rutherman queried.

"Paul Revere?" Jill answered with some hesitation in her voice.

"That's right!" Mrs. Rutherman replied. Jane was proud of the students in her class because she felt that they already had learned so much history since the start of school only 3 weeks ago—with the exception of Felicia, that is. "Felicia, please sit up!" Ms. Rutherman said in a quiet voice so as not to call attention to the student. Ms. Rutherman knew that she somehow lost young Felicia in her quest to teach history to the entire class, but she also did not see how she could individualize her instruction for just one student.

Writing notes on the board as she lectured, Ms. Rutherman noticed that while Felicia had managed to stay awake, she did not copy very many notes down in her notebook. When Ms. Rutherman walked around the room to monitor students' note-taking, she saw Felicia's pages covered with the names of famous rock bands and the words *History died. Let's move on.* As Mrs. Rutherman finished her lecture the bell rang, but before students could leave, she reminded them about the Monday quiz. Almost all of the students made a note of this on their papers, except Felicia, who closed her book and walked out of class. After Felicia left class, Ms. Rutherman asked herself, "What can I do to get this student involved?"

BACKGROUND INFORMATION

Jane was starting her second year of teaching. After a successful first year, she was poised and confident as she taught. Although much of the class time was spent lecturing, her enthusiasm for history had helped to keep the discussions and lectures lively. Students asked questions about information that they did not understand, and Jane provided imaginative stories about actual events. The give-and-take of this style of presenting information had made Jane one of the best first-year history teachers in the district. Despite her pride in her teaching and her contagious enthusiasm, at the end of the day she would become upset about the one or two students whom she could not reach. Felicia was one of them. Only 3 weeks into the semester, Felicia had earned a C and a D on the two announced quizzes.

Jane, concerned about Felicia, began to ask herself a series of questions: "Was Felicia lazy?" "Does Felicia have a learning or reading problem?" "Can Felicia take notes?" "Does Felicia study for the quizzes?" The next day Jane decided to look over Felicia's school records. To her amazement, Felicia's IQ was listed as 127, and her grades had been average to above average over the past 3 years. She then checked with Felicia's other teachers to find that she had started the school year off very poorly in most of her subjects, a dramatic change from her prior performance. Armed with this information, she decided to schedule an after-class meeting with Felicia.

That next day when class had finished, Jane asked Felicia to stay after so that she could talk to her. Felicia agreed, and the two sat down at a large table in the back to talk.

"Look, Felicia, I know that you are an intelligent girl. I can't understand why you don't pay attention in my class. Your records show that you are a good student," Ms. Rutherman said.

Felicia was slow to respond, but eventually spoke up and said, "History is a real drag, and your voice just puts me to sleep."

Ms. Rutherman, trying to hold back her amazement at Felicia's candid response, followed up with another question, "Well, what don't you like about history or the way I teach it?" Felicia, feeling uncomfortable, replied, "Let's just face it. I don't like you and you don't like me. End of story."

Ms. Rutherman wanting to avoid a confrontation, tried to change the subject by asking about Felicia's home, "Is there something going on at home that I should know about?"

To that question, Felicia quickly responded, "It's none of your damn business! I'm outa here!" Felicia then took off for the door.

As she walked out, Ms. Rutherman yelled, "If you fail history, you'll have to repeat it this summer." Then Ms. Rutherman murmured under her breath, "History repeating itself." With the irony of that statement, Jane sat in her chair and shook her head. Reflecting on their conversation, she wasn't certain how well she had done or what step to take next. Jane had thought of calling Felicia's mother, Rosie, but her experiences with Lucia, Felicia's older sister, had prevented the phone call. Jane had had similar problems with Lucia and had tried to contact her mother, but after three attempts, she had been unable to contact her. She then tried to mail a letter to her house, but it was returned as undeliverable. So she gave up on Lucia, who ended up passing with a C-. Perhaps there was still hope for Felicia.

Once at home, Felicia complained to Lucia that the "history Nazi" is giving her a hassle. Felicia's sister, a senior in high school, dislikes most of her teachers and is wary of adult authority figures. She too has confrontations with her teachers, and so she empathizes with Felicia's problems. As her role model, Lucia has taught Felicia how to smoke marijuana and drink hard liquor. For Felicia, these "escapes" are just the thing to do on weekends. Felicia, although a good student, can't see the connection between history (as well as other school subjects) and her vocational goal of working at the Farside Music store. Felicia's love for rock music has helped her to set this rather humble goal.

After school, Felicia often turns up the speakers and listens to music with her sister, before their parents arrive home. At her sister's prodding, Felicia has smoked marijuana on a number of occasions. As she smokes, she imagines herself partying with Benji "Gimme" Moore, the lead drummer of Dead Cat Skins. As she likes to say, "Life is a party. Drink while you can and to hell with school, to hell with the world" (the lyrics from the *Blown Away* album by the Dead Cat Skins).

CASE **14**

HOMEWORK TIME

 ## THE INCIDENT

Gretchen Schmitz plopped down on the couch and closed her eyes. It had been a long day at the office and the evening battle over homework was yet to begin. Within seconds, the briefcase had slipped from Gretchen's hands to the floor as she drifted into sleep. Her husband, Charley, was away on business all week. Her 10-year-old son, also named Charley, was upstairs in his bedroom playing video games and hoping his mother wouldn't call out those dreaded words: "Homework time!"

When Gretchen awoke, it was almost 8 o'clock, long past the official 7 o'clock start of homework time for little Charley. Gretchen walked up the stairs to find Charley still playing video games. She sighed. She hadn't really expected to see him proposed up at his desk with his pencil grinding away on tonight's math problems. For once, though, it would be nice if he would take responsibility for his own homework.

"Let's go, champ." Gretchen motioned Charley to his desk and pulled up a second chair for herself. She sat down.

Charley left the video game running and jumped onto his bed. Rolling up in his covers, he groaned, "Oh, Mom, not again."

"Yes, again," Gretchen could feel her internal thermometer rising. She had little patience for this nightly tussle. "And again and again and again. How do you think your father and I got to where we are today? We did our homework every night for twelve years, then four more, then even more after that."

Charley wrapped the pillow around his head and ignored his mother's words. He repeated softly, "And law school is the most difficult of all, most difficult of all, most difficult of all."

Gretchen took three deep breaths. She felt the growing tension in her forehead and reminded herself that she had had a long day at work. She could envision herself about to snap, about to start shouting and grabbing little Charley by the arm. She closed her eyes and took two more deep breaths and imagined herself sitting on the Adirondack chair on the back porch of their weekend cottage. The breeze through the pines was soft and fragrant. Finally, she opened her eyes and said, "Okay, Charley, we up the ante."

"Up?" Charley's face popped up from behind the pillow. "How much?"

"We'll double it. That's 20 cents a problem for math and 30 cents per comprehension question in reading. But that's only for correct answers."

"I know," Charley said as he leaped out of bed and rushed over to his desk. He imitated his father's deep voice, " 'Nobody pays anyone to do a job poorly.' " With that, Charley quickly opened his reading text and began to read the assigned story in his reading book.

BACKGROUND INFORMATION

The Schmitz household runs on a very tight schedule. Gretchen and Charley are both successful lawyers for a major firm. They drive each morning from their large suburban home into the downtown business district. Generally only one of the two parents is able to come home in time to pick up little Charley at the sitter's house and supervise his homework. Because both parents have more than ample work responsibilities, they often squabble over who can work late and who must go home to pick up their son. Gretchen often finds herself fulfilling the child-care role, thereby sacrificing some of her career aspirations and allowing her husband a greater chance to excel at the firm. She has mixed emotions about doing this. She feels her heart pull her toward her son, while she also silently resents the assumed gender roles played out in the arrangement. Because of his parents' demanding schedules, little Charley almost always eats dinner at the sitter's house.

The Schmitzes were both excellent students throughout their many educational years. They have difficulty comprehending their son's reluctance to do academic work and his evident struggles to do well.

Little Charley is a fourth grader at the Clifton School, a small and expensive private school. His teachers have consistently expressed concern that Charley's reading skills have been developing slowly. Recent testing places his reading decoding and comprehension skills in the second-grade range, a markedly low score for a student at Clifton. His mathematics scores are average for his age, and his general informational knowledge is well above average.

At the most recent parent-teacher conference, Ms. Curwin, Charley's teacher, hesitantly voiced the possibility of a learning disability to Charley's mother. The professionals at Clifton often feel pressure to deliver high achievement from students because the students' parents are generally highly educated and financially successful. Suggesting that a parent seek testing for a learning disability is very difficult for the teachers to do. Additionally, knowing that they work in a school with an extremely low teacher-student ratio and the best curricular materials and educational technology available, the teachers take enormous personal responsibility for their students' learning. They are very slow to suggest that a child may have a learning disability.

Ms. Curwin's words, "learning disability," flew right past Ms. Schmitz as she quickly stated that Charley would simply work harder. She and her husband tend to downplay the extent of Charley's academic weaknesses, assuming instead that he is a late bloomer who will soon "grow out of it."

The evening struggle over homework has blossomed into a tremendous nightly headache for both mother and son. Two weeks before the incident detailed here, Gretchen called Ms. Curwin to seek her advice. How could she get Charley to do his homework without a nightly battle? Ms. Curwin suggested using a behavior modification program through which Charley would earn small rewards for completing his homework.

Gretchen pulled out her old psychology textbook from college and read the section on behavior modification. She set up a reinforcement system whereby Charley would receive 1 point for each school assignment completed. When he had saved up 25 points, he would earn the new video game he has been begging for recently, "Night of the Frog Ranger." Unfortunately, this plan only held Charley's interest for five evenings. On the sixth evening, Charley counted his points and moaned. "This deal isn't fair. It'll take me to forever to get the Frog Ranger." This complaint sparked an argument between the mother and son about the fairness of the reward system.

Gretchen was frustrated. They used to argue over the homework itself. Now they had "progressed" to arguing about the reinforcers. She observed that Charley seemed more interested in sustaining the conflict with his parents than in earning the game. Additionally, she wondered if earning rewards was all that appealing anyway. She had to admit that her son already owned so many toys that his room could hardly contain them. Why would the kid who has everything want to earn more stuff?

Exasperated, Gretchen turned to her husband, who declared, "Forget the points. No one wants to earn points. Pay him cash. I work for money. You work for money. Let him work for money." The next day Gretchen started paying little Charley for completing his homework. The effectiveness of financial rewards has been inconsistent. Some evenings little Charley is excited about earning the cash. Other nights he seems not to care about earning rewards.

Gretchen decided to set up a meeting with Ms. Curwin to seek additional advice. Perhaps they were doing the reinforcement program in the wrong way. The way the psychology textbook explained behavior modification made it seem highly precise and technical. Maybe they were doing it wrong. Gretchen also wondered if perhaps a different approach to changing Charley's behavior would be more effective.

CASE **15**

IMAGE MANAGEMENT

 ## THE INCIDENT

"Tyler, this is the third time they've sent you to see me this month," Mr. Secaucus wheezed in a foghorn voice through the midnight darkness of his office. He fingered the edges of a manila file and occasionally peered at the paper contents. Tyler, the accused tenth grader, sat across from the guidance counselor's desk. His black leather biker's jacket squeaked as he shifted nervously about in the tiny chair provided for him. Occasionally his left hand toyed with a small gold ring that looped through the side of his nose. The blinds were drawn tightly to hold out the sunlight. Only a small desk lamp located midway between the counselor and student cast light upon the situation.

"Um . . . Four."

"What?"

"Mr. Secaucus," Tyler corrected the veteran counselor, "I think this is the fourth time."

"Really?" The counselor leaned his large, round face into the light and pulled his reading glasses down to the tip of his nose. "You say four?"

"Well, there were three times for skipping detention. I mean, I skipped twice for each time. Six total skips, but you don't get sent to the Big Tuna—I mean, to see you, uh, unless you skip twice."

"And what did you get those three detentions for in the first place? I don't recall." Mr. Secaucus settled his large body back in his chair and laughed to himself. He hadn't heard that "Big Tuna" nickname since the early eighties.

"Smoking in the boys' room. Coach Wilkes likes to catch me between second and third period." Tyler smiled hesitantly. He seemed to be gaining a little confidence as the session progressed.

"Coach likes to catch you and you like to get caught?"

"I need the cigarette, you know. And it seems to make his day to catch me. Like, if he can't win enough football games, at least he's nailing me to the wall."

Mr. Secaucus chuckled. "I'm glad to hear you feel some indebtedness to our beleaguered football coach. I guess someone *should* bolster his self-esteem a bit after last year's loss to Lakeville."

"And Southside, Phillipsburg, East Ridge—"

"Okay, Tyler, I get the point. Coach Wilkes can definitely use a little pick-me-up to help his damaged spirits. I'm just wondering why it has to be you."

"Just trying to do my community service, I guess."

"Uh-huh. I see." The counselor paused for a second to consider the situation. He was well aware that Tyler's older brother Kelly was star halfback for the football team. Kelly was well known in this small-town high school as the proverbial Big Man on Campus; a star athlete, favorite of the girls, and National Honor Society student. In contrast, Tyler seemed like a confused Thug Wannabee with a new nose ring and a cheap leather jacket. One could never tell whether Tyler was actually heading down the wrong path or simply trifling with trouble in order to cultivate a tough-guy image. "Well," Mr. Secaucus continued, "What is this fourth offense that brings you to me today?"

"Ms. West caught me trying to leave the school grounds."

"You were skipping her class again?"

"Hey, how'd you know—I mean, yeah, not *again*, really. Not like I'm not there all the time. I'm almost always in Ms. West's class."

Mr. Secaucus peered through his reading glasses at the folder in his hands. It was too dark to read. He leaned forward under the desk lamp to read the file. "It says here that you've missed Ms. West's third-period class fifteen times in the past four months. Your grades have dropped markedly in English and history. What's the deal? I thought she was your favorite. She helps you keep up in your other classes. Without her, you'd be sunk."

Tyler shrugged his shoulders with an odd grin. "I guess so. I'm sinking all right."

"Tyler, you've got to be sinking for Ms. West to write you up. She's the last one to write up a disciplinary action on a student. She must be worried to death about you."

The accused and the counselor sat for a minute in the darkness. Tyler alternately smiled as if he were pulling a fast one and frowned the worrisome frown of a small boy who is about to disappoint his parents again. Mr. Secaucus rummaged through his files for Tyler's home phone number. He punched the digits on the phone and wondered silently why this boy was making such an extreme but only partially successful effort to seem nonchalant in the midst of obvious failure.

BACKGROUND INFORMATION

It would be an understatement to say that the 308 students of Polk High School know each other. They know each other in that intimate, rumor-filled, supportive yet style-cramping way that only happens in a small mountain town. On Friday nights, you can be sure to find every citizen at the high school football game, cheering on the Polk Panthers, grumbling about bad officiating, and catching up on the news of the past week. On Sunday morning the bleach-pale coal miners, dressed in snug suits wearing thin at the elbows, humbly line the church pews with their wives and children. Then they go off to the pancake house or nearby Morrison's Cafeteria for a brunch that could satisfy Goliath.

Clyde and Delores Eldredge have two sons, Tyler and Kelly. Clyde is well liked around town. He owns and operates the Krispy Kreme donut store on the corner of Main and Jefferson. He is past president of the school board and current leader of the Polk Chamber of Commerce. He is considered the "salt of the earth," a regular kind of guy who will happily refill your coffee while you gripe about the government or lend a pickup truck and a helping hand when you can't fit all that firewood you bought into the back of your own truck.

Few people in Polk would call Clyde an alcoholic. Friends would prefer instead to say that he likes a cold beer now and then. Truthfully, Clyde has struggled with an alcohol abuse problem for years. He tends to be a quiet, solitary sort of drunk who stays at home and drinks beer while he fiddles with half-completed projects in his garage workshop. His family and friends have helped him to conceal this difficulty and remain in the good graces of the community that praises him. In the last 6 months, since Dolores finished her associate's degree and started attending Long Notch College, Clyde's drinking has increased noticeably. Although he has not complained, Clyde has felt betrayed by Dolores's extensive time out of the home and her obvious success in an academic world far beyond his tenth-grade education.

When the boys were little, Dolores was a stay-at-home kind of mom. Once the boys reached high school, she found herself getting restless in the big empty house, so she started taking courses at the community college. Now she drives over an hour each way to take courses at the 4-year college on the other side of the mountain. She hopes to earn a degree in journalism and write for the town newspaper.

The sibling rivalry between 17-year-old Kelly and his 16-year-old brother Tyler has never been obvious. The boys played well together as youngsters. Once Kelly reached junior high school, the two boys seemed to go their separate ways. Kelly climbed to the top of every achievement mountain in sight. He excelled in academics and sports. In contrast, Tyler found reading and writing to be nearly impossible chores. He and his mother would sit at the kitchen table for long hours each evening, his eyes poring over the strange shapes on the page, his mouth endlessly repeating initial consonant sounds. The two ended up in tears and arguments on many evenings.

Tyler was diagnosed with a learning disability in the fifth grade. At that time, testing indicated that his reading and writing skills were two to three grade levels behind those of his classmates. He received extra help in a resource room throughout his junior high school years. His literacy skills improved very slowly. He struggled in all academic areas except mathematics and music. With his parents' support and divine auditory patience, he took up the drums. They bought him a drum kit and he practiced each night in the basement. By the time he entered Polk High School, Tyler had written off the academic world as personally unfulfilling while excelling as drummer for both the school marching band and award-winning jazz band.

At Polk High School, Tyler is taking the standard tenth-grade classes. The learning disabilities program at Polk consists of a resource class that operates like a rolling study hall. Ms. West is the teacher, a veteran of 16 years in the classroom.

She likes to keep her resource room low-key and relaxed. Students are typically assigned to her class for one or two periods per day. They enter, sit wherever they want, and work on assignments for their "mainstream" classes. Ms. West views herself as an all-purpose tutor who can help students on an as-needed basis. Often students need assistance understanding the material presented in class or in the subject area texts. Ms. West has worked many hours to produce detailed outlines of text chapters in the various subject areas. Also, she helps students study for tests. Many of her students can grasp the conceptual and factual content of American history or biology but cannot demonstrate this knowledge on the tests.

Tyler is assigned to attend Ms. West's class third period each day. His attendance and effort over the past year have been inconsistent. At times, he has worked closely with Ms. West. She has taught him note-taking and test preparation skills. He has benefited from a small English study group, a group of three tenth-grade boys who help each other comprehend and analyze the complex pieces of literature required for class.

CASE 16

A BLUE INK LINE

THE INCIDENT

Six of the eight students in Mr. Rose's class were working quietly. Little Dougie was toying with something in his desk, probably an eraser shaped like a super-hero or a race car with battery-operated lights that shone clear to the back of his desk. Mr. Rose ignored him for the moment. His attention was captivated by Celia as she struggled with her spelling assignment. She was working very hard, but not very quietly. Her face was red and tense. Every 5 seconds or so she sighed or moaned. Occasionally she struck her fist against the side of her leg. Mr. Rose rolled his teacher's chair up to the 9-year-old's desk.

"You seem a little frustrated. Can I give you some help?"

"This book is so stupid." the exasperated youngster replied. "Stooo-pid. Stooo-pid. Stoooo-pid."

"What don't you understand?" asked the teacher.

"All of it. It's so stupid. Stooo-pid!" Celia rapped her pencil nervously against the desk as she spoke.

Mr. Rose leaned in to examine her paper. She had spelled the first eight words correctly. On number 9, she had incorrectly written "avenue" as A-V-A-N-U-E. As Mr. Rose reached his pen across to write on her paper, she gasped. She quickly pushed his hand aside. His pen had made a half-inch blue ink line on her paper. She rubbed the line furiously with her pencil eraser, but it would not come out. Then she burst into tears.

"You ruined it! You ruined it!" she cried.

"Celia," Mr. Rose attempted to calm her, "It's OK. It's only a little line."

"No! You ruined it! Why did you do that? You ruined everything!" she shouted repeatedly, the tears rolling down her angry face. She jumped out of her seat and snatched up her chair. She held her chair over her head. Mr. Rose backed away. She stepped toward him, a tiny girl carrying a large chair. She repeatedly threatened, "I'm going to hurt you. I'm going to break your head."

BACKGROUND INFORMATION

Celia is a student at the Durham School, a public school day-treatment program for students diagnosed with severe emotional and behavioral disorders. She entered the program only 1 week before this incident. That week had passed without an apparent problem, although Mr. Rose noticed that Celia seemed obsessive and perfectionistic in regard to both her appearance and the orderliness of her possessions. For example, she had a particular place in her desk for her pencil box, her notebooks, her textbooks, and her hairbrush. She also did not like her peers to touch her, even if only by accident. She would quickly complain if someone bumped her in the water fountain line after gym class.

Prior to admission to the Durham School, Celia reportedly had many behavior problems at both school and home. These problems seemed to reached a crescendo in recent weeks when Celia experienced a number of disruptive episodes in school. Her third-grade teacher had finally realized that she simply didn't know how to run a safe and positive learning environment with Celia in the class. On three occasions, Celia exploded into a rage, flipping her desk upside down, tossing her books about the room, and shouting obscenities at her teacher.

Throughout the year, Celia had been very stubborn, often refusing to follow her teacher's directions or mumbling under her breath in response to those directions. There were days when Celia's mood seemed fixed and negative, when she wouldn't allow anyone to tell her what to do. Her teacher, Ms. Stanfield, coped with Celia's moods by allowing her freedom to choose her activities. If the class was working on a social studies lesson and Celia refused, Ms. Stanfield allowed Celia to choose another activity. Ms. Stanfield was pleased if the rest of the group could go on with their work while Celia busied herself with her own choice. This tactic had been effective, due primarily to the fact that while Celia could be very obstinate, she was far from lazy. She enjoyed keeping herself busy. If given a choice of activities, she quickly picked one and buried herself in the work.

In Celia's final month in the general education class, Ms. Stanfield observed that Celia's tension and anger seemed heightened, as if something were making every little conflict and problem rise to heightened urgency. Negotiating the choice of activities with Celia, previously a quick and simple task, had become as difficult as management-union negotiations during a strike. Celia balked and wrangled over the choices. She complained that the choices were no good. She seemed to want to engage her teacher in an angry conflict.

Additionally, while Celia had not been a particularly close friend with her classmates, she seemed further estranged from the group. Ms. Stanfield began to hear reports from two girls that Celia pushed them and threatened to hurt them.

At home, Celia lives with her mother Terese, her father Will, and her 6-year-old sister Candace. Will works long hours as a line repairman for the local electric company. He generally remains silent during mettings with school personnel, allowing his wife to speak for him. Terese is a hair stylist. She is very worried about

Celia's behavior. She sometimes thinks that Celia's behavior must be due to her own incompetence as a mother.

Candace has apparently not had behavior problems, though Celia's parents report that Celia and Candace often argue and fight. Candace is often the target of Celia's anger. The girls' parents admit that Candace provokes Celia, but they generally claim that Celia is the center of the problem.

Terese and Will have been married for 10 years. They report that their marriage and home life have been happy until Celia's recent instances of misbehavior. In the past 3 months, Terese has had increasing difficulty getting Celia to comply with her mother's directions. For example, one evening when Will was working late, Terese decided to take the two girls shopping at the supermarket. As they shopped, Celia refused to stay by her mother's side. She wandered the store on her own. When the time came to load the groceries in the car and go home, Celia would not get in the car. Terese and Celia had a 20-minute standoff in the parking lot. Celia repeatedly stated that she would only get in the car if she got the front seat and her younger sister rode in the back. Because it was Candace's turn to sit up front, Terese would not give in to Celia's demands. Celia's talk soon deteriorated from demanding the front seat to saying that she wouldn't ride unless they left Candace behind. Finally, after 20 minutes of embarrassment in the middle of the busy parking lot, Terese let Celia ride up front. Candace cried all the way home, and Terese felt she was failing as a mother.

Terese and Will are hopeful about Celia's behavior and emotional state improving at the Durham School, a well-staffed, therapeutic program for troubled youngsters in grades K–5. The program consists of six classrooms of eight students, each staffed by a special education teacher and an aide. The support staff includes a crisis teacher who helps individual teachers handle behavior outbursts and instances of conflict in the classroom. Additionally, the school is served by two professionals with mental health training, a guidance counselor and a social worker. These professionals provide group therapy for the students, consult with teachers on issues of emotion and behavior, and work with parents on dealing with family problems. The principal of the Durham School views himself as a hands-off manager whose job is to handle the bureaucratic red tape in order that his staff may do as they see fit.

Although the Durham School staff holds the overall goal of preparing troubled students to reenter the general education mainstream, they are rarely successful in doing so. Less than 10% of their students ever return to general education classrooms. The teachers and support staff blame this fact on the severity of the students' emotional and behavioral problems, the lack of effort on the part of many parents to work closely with the school, and the reluctance of general education teachers and building principals to give troubled students a second chance.

WHEN A JOKE IS NO LONGER A JOKE

THE INCIDENT

"When was the last time Ms. Drudge had a man?" Betty whispers across the class-room to Joan and Eddie.

Interested, but wanting to avoid trouble, the two students silently mouth, "I don't know. When?"

"The night after she got her first set of wooden teeth," Betty responds. A handful of students laugh half-aloud. Ms. Drudge, busy writing notes on the board, turns around and tells the class to be quiet. Betty remains quiet for a few minutes, but then cracks another joke. The students seated near her again laugh at her joke. Ms. Drudge, trying to ignore the behavior, continues working at the board. A third time Betty makes another joke and again the class laughs. Ms. Drudge again ignores the laughter. Within minutes, Betty makes a silly face behind Ms. Drudge's back and again the class laughs. This time, Ms. Drudge points to Betty and says "Quiet down." Betty is silent for a few minutes, but then she thinks of another joke.

Betty makes a face and comments, "I need a fix. I have a Drudge problem." Her classmates again roar. When Ms. Drudge looks for the guilty party, students' eyes point in Betty's direction. This little scenario repeats itself three times until Ms. Drudge finally sends Betty into the hall.

BACKGROUND INFORMATION

Although it is only the second week of classes, Betty has been in trouble a number of times. Betty enjoys being the class clown, but often pays the price—her parents ground her for a day or two for each school incident. She has been the class clown for a number of years and in the process has managed to cause havoc for many of her teachers. At home, even as a child, Betty would often put on evening "shows" consisting of dances, songs, jokes, and exaggerated imitations of famous movie stars. She entertained her mother for hours. Humor runs in the family. Her mother's witty sarcasm and her father's unequaled comedic timing have combined to produce a very funny little girl.

The very funny girl has a hidden, dark secret: depression.

Perhaps it is through her humor that Betty has creatively struggled through her deep bouts of melancholy, hopelessness, and lethargy. Diagnosed with a chronic, moderate form of depression since the age of 11, Betty has managed the various depressive symptoms through a combination of medication, humor, and support. Her parents, Phil and Mill Parot, have provided tremendous love and support through the years. They have taken Betty to various doctors in an attempt to find the optimal treatment for her.

Now 15, Betty currently uses a three-pronged treatment regimen to manage her depression. She takes an antidepressant medication, attends weekly group therapy, and uses conflict resolution techniques to deal with interpersonal conflicts with family members or friends. In the past, there were quite a few dark days. Her parents can recall when Betty would stay in bed for a week on end, even though her parents tried to coax her to eat some soup, play a game of Spades, or watch a video.

Then there were the times when she would use alcohol and illegal drugs in an attempt to alleviate her feelings of sadness and anxiety. Her use of drugs and alcohol only lasted for 2 years, her seventh and eighth grade, and now she does not use either. There are still some days when Betty remains in her dark bedroom under the covers, refusing to speak to anyone. Betty refers to these days as the "demon days." She jokingly claims to have been possessed by dark demons who steal her spirit. Although she uses this analogy in figurative terms, her mother can't help but notice that some of those demons seem very real.

Phil and Mill are both glad that Betty is back in school. Although they feel that they have to take some action about Betty's difficulties, they are just happy that Betty is back to "normal." Educated in a regular education classroom, Betty benefits from special consultation services from Norma Gaspin, the special education teacher who works with students with emotional and behavioral disorders. In a unique mainstreaming model, kids with mild disabilities receive almost all of their services in the regular education classroom. Betty tends to do well enough when her mood is up. During depressive cycles, Betty often feels inadequate and unable to keep up with the demands of her classes. Without extra support, she would give up and perhaps even fail. Ms. Gaspin provides extra emotional support, on-the-spot counseling when Betty feels anxious, and academic tutoring to help Betty prepare for tests. Betty tends to become very anxious before tests. She doubts her ability to do well on subject matter that she obviously understands. Ms. Gaspin just provides the little nudge of reassurance that Betty needs to keep her on the right track.

Betty has an IQ slightly above average, but often performs on an average level in her academic work. She has also been tested for learning disabilities, but she did not qualify.

For the most part, Betty's parents and Ms. Gaspin feel that Betty's behavior is like that of most teenagers. Ms. Drudge, on the other hand, is not in agreement. When Betty's parents met Ms. Drudge for the last two meetings, the first words out of Ms. Drudge's mouth were, "In the twenty years that I have been teaching, I have never had a student quite like Betty." Known for her serious, no-nonsense attitude, Ms. Drudge annually ranks as one of the mostly highly rated teachers in the school year after year. She likes to tell parents that she is "tough and effective." She makes students study, complete homework, and take notes: three things that she claims too many schools don't teach and as a consequence results in high student failure. Unfortunately for Betty, her learning style and Ms. Drudge's often successful teaching style clash.

Ms. Drudge has class rules clearly posted on the wall. In plain sight are the following rules: No gum chewing; no talking, unless called upon; no cursing. In addition, all students say "ma'am" or "sir" when addressing adults. The physical layout of her room has the desks are arranged in rows, with just enough room between aisles to allow Ms. Drudge to pass through. Her class schedule is arranged for very little "down time." Her students are always busy either taking notes from her lectures, completing worksheets, or sitting quietly studying alone. When students are finished working, they must do one of two things: quietly work at one of two content review centers or quietly read their library books. For Betty, sitting still in her seat and being quiet are two skills in which she lacks proficiency.

CASE **18**

QUIET FOR JULIA

THE INCIDENT

Julia Whitfield is a 12-year-old student in the self-contained, mild/moderate disabilities classroom at Washmore Elementary School. It is her first day back in class. She has just returned to school after a 1-month psychiatric hospitalization. As she is walking to the lunchroom with the rest of the class, Larry, another student, runs up behind her and calls her "crazy kid." Two other boys join in with taunts of "looney tunes," "crybaby," and "wacky girl." The boys have heard of Julia's psychiatric problems and have placed a bet to see which student will be the first to make her cry. Finally, after hearing someone whisper to her that her mother made her crazy, Julia begins to cry and bolts ahead of the class. By the time Ms. Babson, the teacher, catches up to Julia, she is already in full tears and near hysteria. As Ms. Babson sits down next to her, Julia gets up and runs to another seat, all the while refusing to talk about what has happened.

BACKGROUND INFORMATION

Julia has returned to school after a month-long stay at the residential treatment center known as Quiet Haven. Quiet Haven serves children and adolescents with psychological disorders. In Julia's case, she has just recovered from a bout of severe depression. Now that she is stable, the psychiatrists at Quiet Haven feel that she should return to her regular school.

  She was originally admitted to Quiet Haven shortly after Christmas because her mother said that she was constantly talking about death and suicide. Celia Whitfield noticed that Julia had lost interest in school and social events in early December. Normally, Julia loved the Christmas season. Typically, Julia and a number of her friends would spend evenings at the arcade in the mall where the discussions often centered around boys. However, this December was different. Gone were Julia's friends and her normally joyous mood. Instead, Celia observed Julia to be quite irritable and melancholy. When Celia asked her daughter what was wrong, Julia would often reply, "Nothing" or "Leave me alone." After school, Julia would frequently lock herself in her room and listen to her CDs. As the Christmas season passed, Celia noticed no improvement in Julia; in fact, her daughter seemed to be slipping deeper and deeper into depression.

Often Celia asked Bill, her husband, "What has happened to our daughter?" Bill, an executive with a giant oil company, would simply shrug his shoulders and tell her that it was part of growing up. Working long hours to provide for his family's upper-class lifestyle, Bill was never very involved in Julia's life. Being the vice president of a major corporation left Bill with very little time in the evening to speak to or see his daughter. On weekends, Bill was generally to be found in front of their large-screen TV watching sports. Bill would often admit that his relationship with Julia was at best strained, and he had difficulty talking to her. Bill often remarked, "She talks about girl things. I don't know anything about that stuff."

One of Julia's best friends, Stephanie, stopped by the day after Christmas to listen to some CDs with her and to drop off a gift for Julia. When Stephanie rang the doorbell, Celia answered and was happy to see Stephanie.

"Oh, what a wonderful Christmas surprise!" Celia remarked upon greeting her at the door. She called out to Julia that Stephanie was here to see her, then she whispered in Stephanie's ear that Julia had been feeling down in the dumps recently. As Julia walked down the stairs to greet her friend, it was clear that Stephanie's visit was more of an annoyance than a surprise for Julia.

"Why don't you two girls go to your room to spend some time together," Celia said. Once in Julia's room, Stephanie began to quiz her about her erratic behavior. "Why don't you return my calls? Why are you acting so weird? Why are you always locked up in your room?" These were the first three questions that Stephanie fired at Julia. To each question, Julia had a blank look on her face and replied that she didn't want to deal with people.

Realizing that she had irritated Julia, Stephanie turned the conversation to a new topic. "So, Julia, what are you going to do for the holidays?" asked Stephanie.

To this Julia replied, "I'm going to see Grandpa Joe."

"Oh, you mean, like, his grave?"

"Yeah."

Stephanie sensed that something wasn't right. She inquired further about Julia's deceased grandfather. "What are you going to do that for?"

"Because I wonder what it would be like to be Grandpa Joe, you know, to be dead," replied Julia. Julia and Grandpa Joe had been very close and often spent hours talking about school, friends, and life. When Grandpa Joe died 5 months ago, Julia had been very upset, but seemed to adjust. Throughout their conversation, Stephanie felt uneasy. She wanted to leave but felt compelled to stay. Finally, Stephanie herself began to feel down in the dumps. She abruptly said she had to go home. As Stephanie was leaving the house she remarked to Celia, "That's not the same Julia I knew a month ago."

As Celia closed the door, she too remembered happier times. She recalled how she and Julia used to spend hours hiking in the nearby forest and talking about school. She also recalled how Julia used to love helping her cook and how their conversations would linger well into the evening. Contemplating the changes that she saw in Julia, Celia also felt guilty that she might have inadvertently done something wrong to affect Julia's mood. "Am I too nosy about Julia's problems? Am I being too pushy with Julia?" Celia thought to herself.

The house was quiet. Celia caught the sound of Julia's voice. As she listened intently, she heard Julia crying. Immediately, Celia ran to the top of the stairs and called out, "Julia, sweetie, is everything okay?" Julia did not respond. As Celia got closer to Julia's door, she called out for Julia to open the door so that they could talk. When Julia refused, Celia opened the locked door with a key and found her daughter sitting in the dark, crying.

"Sweetie, you need help," Celia replied. At this, Julia began to cry louder and yell that she wished she were dead. Celia told Julia that they were going to see some doctors who could help her. That night they drove to Quiet Haven and admitted Julia.

During her stay at Quiet Haven, Julia met some new friends and began to show improvement. Over the course of a week she was diagnosed by the staff, and Dr. Chall prescribed the psychiatric drug called Prozac, an antidepressant. Dr. Chall prescribed it to Julia because of her thoughts of suicide, fatigue, changes in sleep, and lack of appetite.

As the day neared for Julia's discharge from Quiet Haven, Dr. Chall informed her parents that Julia was still very fragile and warned them to reduce any stress in Julia's life. Dr. Chall's last words to Julia's parents were, "Don't force her to do any activity that she does not want to do. It is only over time in a very supportive environment that Julia will fully recover."

CASE **19**

GO TO THE OFFICE

THE INCIDENT

A straight and silent row of second graders walked down the right side of the long hallway toward the computer lab. Rashid El-Amin, the tallest boy, walked at the front of the line, his shiny black hair serving as a guiding beacon for the well-trained group of youngsters who obediently followed his lead. Ms. Topfield strode along at the left shoulder of the fifth student. While her students faced forward with their shoulders square, Ms. Topfield constantly twisted her torso around to survey the rear two thirds of the line.

A flutter of laughter was emitted from the rear of the line. This was followed by mumbled words and another full giggle. Ms. Topfield spun around in time to see that it was Kit and Jamal. As is typical of such situations, the teacher did not witness the entire sequence of events but quickly pieced together the scenario based on the evidence available. The first giggle of laughter was Kit. Jamal was standing behind her in the line. Based on previous interactions between the two, Ms. Topfield could reasonably guess that Jamal had probably poked Kit in the shoulder, tugged her hair, or stepped on the back of her sneakers.

When Ms. Topfield first spun around, she saw Kit turning to push Jamal's right hand away. The small girl was walking backward and holding her arms in front of her in a defensive stance. The horseplay was obviously not mean spirited on the part of either child. Both students were smiling. Jamal continued in the game for a moment, his hands held up before him as if he were about to tickle Kit. Upon seeing that his teacher was approaching, Jamal started to lower his hands and retreat from the situation. Just then, Kit, who had been walking backward in order to face Jamal, stumbled over the foot of the child in front of her. She let out a tiny shriek, caught herself with one hand as she fell into the wall, and giggled at her own clumsiness.

"Stop! Line leader, stop, please!" called Ms. Topfield. At the front, Rashid halted, and the line instantly froze. Ms. Topfield walked back toward Jamal and Kit at the rear of the line. She reached one hand forward to help Kit regain her balance. In a moment, both Kit and Jamal were back in line, standing like soldiers with stern faces and straight shoulders.

"What is the positive expectation about walking in the hallway?" the teacher quizzed her class. A hand shot up from the center of the line. Ms. Topfield called on the boy to respond.

"Single file, head behind the head in front of you, and—" The little boy's voice trailed off as he tried to recall the third aspect of the expectation.

"And?" Ms. Topfield prompted him in a soft, encouraging voice.

Five other hands flew up. Ms. Topfield shook her head, and four of the five fell right back down.

"And silent?" the responding boy finally queried in a small voice.

"Yes, Timothy, you are right," Ms. Topfield praised the boy, handing him a small piece of green paper called a ticket. The boy gladly pocketed the ticket. The teacher then instructed her class on the complete expectation: "We walk in single file. We keep our head behind the head in front of us. We are silent. All right, Rashid, turn about. Return to the classroom and we'll give this another try."

Rashid crossed the hallway to the opposite side and led the silent line of students back toward their classroom. The students knew that they would then have another attempt at walking to the computer lab according to schoolwide positive expectations.

Ms. Topfield's students walked quietly and sadly back to their classroom, knowing that they might be losing valuable time in the computer lab. Jamal playfully slipped his foot under Kit's leg, tripping her up slightly at each step. Kit played along, jumping over Jamal's sneaker as though she were dodging cracks in the sidewalk. As the two students entered their classroom, Jamal's foot finally struck Kit firmly on the shin. Their legs tangled together and the boy and girl fell to the floor with a shriek and a gasp.

Background Information

Lanacre Elementary School (K–5), housed in a small building, is located in a suburban school district. Ms. Topfield's actions in this incident followed the school guidelines that were instituted within the Positive Expectations Program (PEP) 6 months earlier. The principal had called in a university consultant due to concerns with the high number of office referrals for instances of inappropriate behavior. The school of approximately 400 students had accumulated an astounding 1,400 office behavior referrals over the course of the previous year. This was a mean of 7.8 office referrals per school day. From the data, it could be determined that a relatively small group of students (22) received a large share of the referrals (74%). Additionally, a small group of three teachers produced over half (56%) of the referrals. Ms. Topfield's referral figures were slightly below average in comparison to the other teachers.

The principal and consultant decided to view this as a broad systemic issue rather than a problem specific to a few students or a handful of teachers. It was agreed that the intervention should include all students. The consultant emphasized that such an intervention could be immediately instituted without a full investigation into the reasons why teachers were sending students to the office in such numbers. This lack of understanding of the roots of the problem concerned the principal, but she agreed nonetheless to move forward with the consultant's intervention plan.

The university consultant suggested the school utilize PEP, a schoolwide system of positive reinforcement designed to clarify the behavioral expectations of the faculty and train the children to follow the expectations. The consultant, school principal, and faculty met a number of times to develop a short but comprehensive list of behavioral expectations for all students. Following are the five behavioral expectations that resulted from the meetings:

1. **F**ollow teacher directions.
2. **O**nly positive touching is allowed.
3. **U**se respectful language.
4. **R**aise your hand before speaking.
5. **B**e silent in the halls and cafeteria.

These guidelines quickly became known by students and teachers as the FOURB. "Follow the FOURB" became the buzz phrase around the hallways of Lanacre.

During the first 2 months of the school year, the teachers continuously repeated and encouraged the five expectations. Small green tickets were handed out as positive reinforcers to students observed following any one of the five expectations. Students accumulated the tickets and traded them on every second Friday for special privileges and activities such as computer game time or a popcorn and video afternoon. After the first 2 months, the tickets were no longer given to students. Teachers continued to praise students who complied with the rules, but no tangible incentives were offered. By design, the school went 3 months without the tickets. Then the teachers brought the reinforcers back for use during the month of February. This was designed to work like a booster shot, a brief refresher course on the FOURB, encouraging students to again focus on following the behavioral expectations.

Following are the per day averages of office referrals over the first 6 months of the school year:

September (tickets used)—6.1

October (tickets used)—4.4

November (no tickets)—3.9

December (no tickets)—4.5

January (no tickets)—3.5

February (tickets used)—4.0

As of late February, the date when the line behavior incident detailed here occurred, the faculty of Lanacre were generally satisfied with the results of the program and wished to continue.

When the PEP was initially presented to the faculty by the consultant, reactions varied. Most of the teachers were pleased to have a concrete program that outlined very precisely what they should do. The authority and expertise of the university consultant brought an air of likely success to the proposed program. Still, this supportive group retained a pragmatic ounce of skepticism, a "wait and see how it works" attitude, while generally embracing the program. Ms. Topfield was one of the "wait and see" teachers.

A small group of teachers made up a rather silent opposition force that did not openly criticize the program in faculty meetings but spoke at length among themselves. This coalition was made up of a trio of teachers who were uncomfortable with the PEP for philosophical reasons. This trio felt that the PEP was too much of a training model that valued an unquestioned form of obedience and uniformity. They sarcastically called the program the "Nineteen Eighty-Four B," after the Orwell novel about a frightening future society of absolute conformity.

Kit and Jamal, the two students involved in the line incident, had responded to the program in very different ways. Jamal had always been a pretty well-behaved student, a child who occasionally fooled around behind the teacher's back but always stayed out of serious trouble. He had never been sent to the office for misbehavior. In contrast, Kit was a very active and verbal child who had originally ranked 15th among students in office referrals. Ms. Topfield found that Kit often became angry and talked back when verbally reprimanded or corrected. When the PEP incentive system was implemented in September, Jamal quickly became one of the highest ticket earners in the school, while Kit earned very few tickets. Ms. Topfield made a special effort to reward Kit with a ticket for the most meager demonstration of meeting the behavioral expectations. Her ticket totals soared through the month of October. Nonetheless, Kit's office referral numbers dropped only slightly over the 6 months. It was evident that the PEP was having an uneven impact on Kit's behavior.

A specific group of students seemed to be untouched by the program. While the schoolwide referral figures dropped significantly, 18 of the 22 students who had been sent to the office most frequently during the prior year continued to receive office referrals at the same high rate.

C A S E **20**

OFF TASK

THE INCIDENT

Mr. Palatino rubbed his hands together nervously. He glanced up at Ms. Sanchez, his co-teacher. She smiled hesitantly across the classroom. Both knew what was on the line. Their supervisor, Principal Estes, was seated at the front of the room with a state-mandated effective teaching evaluation instrument in her hands. The key to her evaluation of their classroom came down to "time on task," the amount of time the students spent actually working on their academic activities, a frequent weakness among the students in the Palatino-Sanchez inclusion class.

Ms. Estes was observing the sixth-grade inclusion class, a pilot program developed by Mr. Palatino and Ms. Sanchez. The two veteran teachers knew that Ms. Estes was a stickler for the old-school teaching style. The students had to be on task, heads down, working on their assignments. This was exactly the difficulty that the Palatino-Sanchez class was experiencing. Mr. Palatino had just finished leading the class in an oral introduction to the social studies lesson. He spoke for 5 minutes, about 3 minutes longer than the students seemed to listen. Their eyes wandered, and a few whispered private comments to their neighbors. Then, as the students turned to page 24 and started on the individual reading and writing in their workbooks, the two teachers circled the room in a constant effort to keep the eyes down and the pencils moving. Despite their physical proximity and their gently spoken prompts to the students, Ms. Estes could see that at any given moment, half of the children were off task. They were silent, but their eyes and minds were wandering from the work at hand. Seeing this, and feeling the pressure of the observation, the two teachers redoubled their efforts, encouraging all to complete the reading assignment and the written activities.

After the lesson, Ms. Estes commented briefly that the air conditioning system was too loud and distracting. Ms. Sanchez agreed, but she took little heart in this excuse.

BACKGROUND INFORMATION

Principal Estes and the faculty of Sennett Center recently came under fire from the central district offices because they were the only school in their small rural district that had not developed at least one inclusion classroom. Ms. Sanchez was teaching a self-contained, cross-categorical special education class for students diagnosed with mild degrees of various disabilities: mental retardation, learning disabilities, and behavior disorders. She and Mr. Palatino had discussed the creation of a team-taught, inclusion classroom with Ms. Estes 2 years earlier. Ms. Estes was very skeptical about the idea. She had heard the hype and the hoopla about inclusion at a number of educational conferences, but she was very suspicious of reform movements. She had seen them come and go over the years. In the end, she was convinced that it always came back to business as usual in her school. She felt that the pull-out model was best for her exceptional students. It had been working fine during her 14 years at the helm. She could see no reason to create an uproar simply because some overly idealistic people behind central administration desks didn't know the realities of educating students with disabilities.

When the superintendent finally gave Ms. Estes no choice, she reluctantly told Ms. Sanchez to move her 11 special needs students into Mr. Palatino's room on a full-time basis. On the first day of school, the superintendent himself was present for the inauguration of the program. He encouraged the two teachers and told them to seek the support of his office if they needed any information or special help. The two teachers, knowing little about team teaching and inclusion beyond the few articles they had read about inclusive programs elsewhere, knew that they were initiating a mixed blessing. Supposedly, they had the full support of the fairly inaccessible superintendent's office. They knew he was cheering for them, but he had offered them no special training in preparation for the venture. Meanwhile, they knew that their own Principal Estes would undoubtedly be watching them with a skeptical eye, looking for an opportunity to demonstrate the ineffectiveness of the inclusion model. Needless to say, the two teachers felt enormous pressure.

The one sure benefit of the superintendent's endorsement was that Mr. Palatino and Ms. Sanchez were allowed to interview prospective students' parents before placing the students in the class, in order to guarantee full parental support for the inclusion program. Before the school year began, the two teachers met with every parent to explain the program and to hear the parents' hopes and misgivings. They interviewed all the students' parents, working under the principle that participation in the special program must be voluntary. No parents would be forced to put their child in their class. They arrived at the final group of 25 students, 14 general education and 11 exceptional education students.

The class was as eclectic a group of children as one could find in this relatively homogeneous rural school. The local population was more than 95% White; it consisted of farmers, factory workers, and a sprinkling of Mexican migrant worker families that typically moved about as the various crops required. The inclusion class was populated with general education third graders and special education students who ranged from third grade to fifth grade. The class was balanced in terms of gender. The general education group had six Mexican students with limited English proficiency. Both Ms. Sanchez and Mr. Palatino spoke passable Spanish and felt able to work with these students.

The special education contingent was made up of boys who had spent the previous years in a self-contained special education class at the elementary school. They had become comfortable with each other and with the small, segregated setting.

In the first 2 months of school preceding Ms. Estes' evaluation, Ms. Sanchez and Mr. Palatino had already identified a series of major problems needing their attention. First, the two teachers had very different teaching styles. Mr. Palatino tended to run a pretty traditional classroom. Students sit in rows, and the teacher leads whole-class lessons from the front of the room. Students are expected to follow his oral explanations and instructions as he introduces a new concept or skill. Often he writes on the board as he explains or gives directions. This teacher-directed content is typically followed by individual practice activities that students complete using workbooks, worksheets, or their texts.

In contrast, while teaching in the self-contained special education classroom, Ms. Sanchez grew accustomed to using small cooperative groups and tutoring dyads for virtually all of her instruction. Given the wide range of reading and math abilities and frequent disinterest or inattention among her students, she worked hard to design small projects that teams of two to four students could complete in a short period of time. Often these projects were thematic, integrating math skills and writing or bringing together language arts and science. The thematic nature of the activities freed time for Ms. Sanchez to create curriculum on topics of interest to the students. For instance, she developed an extensive, integrated unit on spiders, an area of mutual intrigue to her pack of preadolescent boys. The difficulty Ms. Sanchez experienced in using this approach was that developing group projects for her students often took incredible quantities of her time.

Ms. Sanchez and Mr. Palatino have discussed adding more cooperative group work to their inclusion class day. Mr. Palatino has agreed in principle, but he has understandably hesitated to change the format that he has used for years. Given the evident attention problems of the students, he wonders if a new cooperative grouping approach will only further distract the children. "Won't the cooperative group members just distract each other?"

Additionally, since the inclusion class is located in the room that has long been Mr. Palatino's class, Ms. Sanchez has struggled to feel that the new inclusion class is actually her class. She often feels like a guest, a welcome guest, but a guest nonetheless. Despite the positive working relationship she and her co-teacher share, she is not yet sure to what extent she can suggest and create changes in what still feels like Mr. Palatino's room.

CASE 21

THE ART OF FAIR PLAY

THE INCIDENT

The enormous sliding walls had been pulled to the center of the basketball court, splitting the gymnasium of Tryon Middle School into two somewhat separate rooms. The double gym echoed with the deafening mixture of shouts from the seventh-grade girls playing crab soccer on the one side and the sixth-grade boys' game of kickball taking place on the other. To the uninitiated newcomer, the sound alone was overwhelming.

The boys' kickball game had been under way for 15 minutes without incident when a conflict erupted between Ben and Chris. Ben Kidwell was a runner on second base when a hot squibbler was booted into short left field. As Ben ran to third, he accidentally ran into Chris Kelly, the shortstop for the opposing team. Ben and Chris fell to the floor in a heap. The left fielder scooped up the red kickball and tagged Ben out. Ben hopped to his feet and shouted angrily at Chris, who lay stunned on the floor.

"Jeez, Kelly, what'd you get in my way for?" shouted Ben. Chris jumped up quickly and clenched his fists. Ben seemed surprised by the fact that Chris stood up for himself. Chris was usually a fairly passive and meek boy. Ben took a cautious step back.

Mr. Kishna, the physical education teacher, shouted across the gym, "Come on, Ben, clear the field. You're out. He nailed you fair and square."

Ben walked slowly toward the sideline, seemingly accepting Mr. Kishna's direction. The red kickball had rolled to the sideline and now rested against the bleachers. As Ben reached the bleachers, he picked up the ball and hurled it back onto the field. The ball soared over the pitcher's outstretched hands and struck the unsuspecting Chris Kelly on the side of the face. Chris knew who had thrown it. He turned and began to stride quickly toward Ben. Chris raised his fists and shouted, "Come on, Kidwell, I've had it with you!"

BACKGROUND INFORMATION

After 18 years of trying to run two physical education classes side-by-side in a cramped gym, Mr. Kishna and his physical education department colleagues finally thought they were going to get the athletic facilities that Tryon Middle

School needed. A recent bond referendum in the small town of Tryon had apparently raised enough money for the new athletic complex, complete with two full gymnasiums. However, a lawsuit had been filed by opponents of the referendum, leaving the issue and Mr. Kishna's hopes of developing a quality physical education program in limbo for months. The veteran coach seemed disheartened. Instead of participating in the games and activities with his middle school students, he had taken to sitting quietly on the sidelines. He had regressed from enthusiastically teaching athletic skills to merely tossing a ball onto the court and watching from a distant chair.

Unbeknownst to Coach Kishna at the time of the kickball game, the conflict that erupted between Ben and Chris had roots in earlier interactions between the two boys. Two days prior to this incident, Ben and Chris occupied seats in the front office, each waiting a turn to speak to Mr. Cole, the assistant principal, about unrelated disciplinary matters. Of the two boys, Ben was far more comfortable with being sent to the office. Due to his often disruptive behavior in class and on the bus, he was a veteran of many disciplinary meetings in his 6 short years of schooling.

On the other hand, Chris was unaccustomed to getting into any trouble at all. This was the first time he had ever been sent out of class for misbehavior. He had been sent to the office for fooling around too much in science class. Whereas Ben felt a certain pride in being sent to the office one more time, Chris felt ashamed. He worried that his parents would find out. He shivered. Sensing Ben's feelings of humiliation, Ben began picking on Chris. He played on Chris's fear and sadness and tried to make him fear the assistant principal all the more.

"Whatcha up for, Kelly?" Ben asked as the two waited on the bench outside Mr. Cole's office.

"I was just making jokes. I wouldn't do it again," Chris confessed with a guilty sigh.

"Jokes, huh?" Ben shook his head from side to side. "You know what Old Man Cole does to jokers?"

"No. What's he do?"

"All I can say is, I wouldn't want to be you. That's all."

Chris's anxiety was rising like floodwaters during the monsoon season. "Why? What do you mean? He's got to be fair. I mean, they got a law about him having to be fair."

"Fair?" Ben laughed and leaned back with a smile. He stuck a pencil in his mouth and pretended to coolly smoke a cigarette.

"Cole's got his own idea of fair."

"Like what? Tell me what you mean!"

"Well, for one thing, Cole's not running a court or nuthin'. He knows you're guilty even before he talks to you. Second, he calls your mother, tells her all about what you done, playin' it up like it's much worse than the real thing. He gets her crying by telling her this will be a, let's see, 'a dreadful mark on Chris's permanent record.' That's how he puts it. He gets her all crying like you're on your way to leading a life of crime. Then he makes you apologize on the phone to her. You ever try to apologize to your mom while she's crying hysterically?"

By the time Chris entered Mr. Cole's office, Ben had worked him up into such a frenzy that Chris walked into the assistant principal's office, sat down, and just cried like a baby. It took Mr. Cole 15 minutes to convince Chris that nothing bad would happen to him.

Indeed, Mr. Cole did not call Chris's mother. He talked briefly to Chris about his behavior in science class, encouraging him to keep up his usual hard work and positive attitude, and sent him on his way. As he walked past the widely grinning Ben on his way out of the assistant principal's office, Chris realized that he had been hoodwinked. Ben had played him for a fool. Chris shot an angry face at Ben and wondered what he could do to get back at him for what he had done.

CASE 22

SIDE BY SIDE

 THE INCIDENT

Jim and Steven are 3-year-old boys playing in the sandbox. Each pushes a yellow truck though the thick sand, around his own legs, over molehills, and along the wooden rail that encloses the sand. The boys aren't really playing together. They seem to be playing side by side, roaring engine sounds in unison but otherwise keeping their truck-driving activities separate.

There are three other youngsters on the small playground of Happy Times Preschool, a special program for young children with disabilities or developmental delays. Two children are standing at the back fence, staring curiously and fearfully at a mound of crawling ants that has sprung up over the weekend. They step on the moving mound and jump back with little shouts of exuberance. The fifth student is Josh, a 4-year-old youngster who suffered a severe brain injury as an infant. He does not speak or seem to understand any language. He sits alone, curled up in a semifetal position, on the bench just outside the classroom door. He rocks slightly, sucks his thumb, and hums to himself.

Ellen Palliser, the teacher, and Pam Hsu, the classroom aide, are rushing about, attending to the million and one details of Monday morning arrival time. Ellen is standing at the front curb by the entrance, greeting parents and children as they pull up. This morning she is helping Dr. Sanchez try to operate the wheelchair lift on her van so that her daughter Tina can roll off the van and into the school. Dr. Sanchez struggles with the awkward mechanism. It is her husband's van and she doesn't know how to work the lift. Mr. Sanchez usually delivers Tina to school, but he is home in bed with the flu, leaving Ellen and Dr. Sanchez to figure out how to get Tina off the van.

Pam, feeling rushed by the sudden arrival of her students, moves quickly back and forth between the small playgound and the classroom. She is attempting to monitor the students who are entering the classroom and the five already on the playground. She tries to rush the arriving students out onto the playground so that she will only have to monitor one area. The students move slowly, so she is, for now, stuck with watching children in two places at once. With each hurried pass through the open doorway, she briefly rubs little Josh on the head, attempting to console him. He looks as if he could use some comfort. On Monday mornings he

108

often cries and screams as his mother leaves him with his teachers and drives away. He seems to go through a new separation process every week. Pam can't wait until she gets a few minutes to sit with him, hold him, and sing him a song. That usually does the trick.

Back in the sandbox, Jim accidentally runs his truck over Steven's hand. Without hesitation, Steven smashes his truck into the rear of Jim's truck. Steven laughs. Jim pulls his hand away, as if frightened. He turns his back to Steven and plays with his truck on the opposite side of the sandbox. Steven then rams his truck into Jim's back. A look of pain comes across Jim's face. As Steven winds up to land another blow, Jim says "no" and reaches out his hand to try to stop the truck from hitting him again. Steven swings the truck forcefully, crashing though Jim's fingers and opening a small cut on the palm of his hand. Jim sees the blood and starts to cry.

" 'Tupid," says Steven in response to Jim's crying.

Pam Hsu has seen this incident from the doorway, where she had paused to tickle Josh. She rushes across the playground to intervene.

BACKGROUND INFORMATION

Ellen has noticed that Steven's maternal grandparents have dropped him off and picked him up for 4 days in a row. Ellen already knew that Steven's parents were embroiled in a very difficult divorce, including a bitter and expensive struggle for custody of Steven and his older sister, Rachel. Although Steven's mother has temporary custody of the children, they have recently been living with their grandparents while she has gone on a business trip to Japan. One afternoon last week, both Steven's father and his maternal grandmother showed up to pick him up in the afternoon. This led to a nasty shouting match between the two on the front steps as other parents and children looked on. Ellen had to explain to Steven's father that she could not release the boy to him because he was no longer the legal guardian. He hopped in his car and tore out of the parking lot with tires squealing.

Steven was admitted to the special program one year earlier due to a significant delay in language development. His general intellectual functioning is considered to be within the typical range. No specific source for his language delay has been found.

Steven's behavior has grown increasingly angry and violent as his parents' divorce and custody battle has dragged on. Even when his parents were together, Steven was a very boisterous boy who loved to roughhouse and tumble around. He seemed to feed off physical play. But he accepted limits set by his teachers and he seemed to want to please adults. Even if a situation made him angry, he would try to follow Pam's or Ellen's directions. In recent days, he has been so angry that he doesn't care very much about how others feel or what others say.

Additionally, in regard to communications about Steven's behavior at Happy Times, Ellen has found Steven's mother very distant and detached. She doesn't seem to want to hear about Steven's difficulties following directions or getting along with the other children. She seems far away, overwhelmed with other issues, as if one more stick on the camel's back would be too much.

Ellen and Pam have been struggling with some problems of their own. Ellen is a veteran preschool teacher who has taught at Happy Times for 10 years. Two years ago, the school district went through a dramatic restructuring and suddenly changed Happy Times to a special education preschool. Ellen was very upset by this program change. She had virtually no experience and even less confidence teaching youngsters with disabilities. The district attempted to comfort her by supplying Pam Hsu, a classroom aide who is both certified and experienced in early childhood special education. Pam accepted the low-paying aide position because she was new to the area and there were no other special education pre-K teaching openings in the district.

Ellen is just now going back for the university courses necessary to add the early childhood special education certification. Her employer gave her 2 years to add this certification. Ellen procrastinated for a year by not taking any classes. Now she is worried that if she doesn't complete her certification on time, the district will hand the Happy Times teaching position to Pam. Silently, and with a fair amount of guilt, Pam hopes to become the teacher at Happy Times.

Needless to say, this has caused a certain amount of tension between the two direct service professionals at Happy Times. Although both teachers are fully aware of this issue and the growing tension between them, the problem has been swept under the rug. As a result, their communication is now minimal and barely cordial. Much like little Steven and Jim in the sandbox, Pam and Ellen tend to work side by side but not really together.

Three weeks ago they received the annual program evaluation report written by Dr. Sara Singh, the district supervisor overseeing Happy Times and a handful of similar early childhood programs. In this evaluation report Dr. Singh wrote:

> Professional communication, a necessity in serving children and their families, has deteriorated in recent months. At times, the classroom is noticeably tense and uncomfortable, possibly influencing the children in ways beyond my observations. In my 4-hour observation on April 18, the teacher and aide spoke to each other 3 times. On interview, neither Ms. Hsu nor Ms. Palliser could offer any reasons why they are not talking to each other. Lacking substantial understanding of the source of the discord, I can merely note that this is an unfortunate decline in communication at a site that has previously been exemplary in all respects. I spoke individually with both Ms. Hsu and Ms. Palliser and encouraged them to improve their communication concerning professional issues.

CASE 23

SKIPPING

THE INCIDENT

"Christy, you can come out for dinner!" Mr. Cleveland called down the hallway. There was no response. An hour earlier, after a loud argument between the father and 13-year-old daughter, Mr. Cleveland sent Christy to her room. Mr. Cleveland had just received a phone call from Mr. Hodapp, Christy's math teacher, informing him that his daughter had already failed math for the quarter due to excessive absences. Mr. Cleveland was shocked and angered. For weeks, Christy had been skipping her math classes, which took place during the final period of the day.

"Christy! Did you hear me?" Mr. Cleveland shouted impatiently. Hearing no reply, he walked quickly down the hallway and knocked on Christy's door. There was no answer. He opened the door to find the room empty. The open window testified to Christy's escape route.

Mr. Cleveland immediately telephoned Christy's best friend, April. When April answered the phone, Mr. Cleveland asked to speak to his daughter. Mr. Cleveland heard the girls' voices in the background, but he couldn't make out what they said. Then April returned to sheepishly pass on a message from Christy.

"She says she can't talk to you right now, Mr. Cleveland. She says she's fine and she'll be home tonight or tomorrow." The line went dead. Mr. Cleveland hung up the phone and sat on the couch to think about the situation.

BACKGROUND INFORMATION

This is the third time Christy has escaped through her bedroom window after being sent to her room. Mr. Cleveland has never believed that sending Christy to her room is an effective disciplinary technique, but it is the only punishment he can think of. The trials of raising an adolescent daughter overwhelm Mr. Cleveland. His little girl is now wearing eye makeup that makes her look like a raccoon, hanging out with ragged-looking boys at the mall, listening to music that sounds like an unending train wreck, and continuously complaining that school is boring.

In the midst of all this, Mr. Cleveland is thankful for the advice and support of Mr. Hodapp, a man who turned out to be not only a good math teacher but also a pretty fair counselor on the exigencies of fathering an adolescent. Mr. Hodapp had demonstrated an early interest in Christy's well-being. At the beginning of the school year, he noticed that Christy had an unusual talent for mathematics, a talent that she seemed to neither notice nor care about. Mr. Hodapp called Mr. Cleveland to suggest that Christy might benefit from joining the Slide Rulers, the math and computer skills club and competition team at the junior high school. Mr. Hodapp has served as faculty sponsor for the club for over 20 years (since the days when the pretechnological moniker wasn't such an anachronism), leading the club to six state titles in math competitions. During this initial discussion, the two men discovered that they had much in common; each was a single parent with a 13-year-old daughter.

Mr. Cleveland looks to the educator for advice in dealing with Christy's behavior problems. Mr. Hodapp emphasizes the need for absolute consistency. Setting a firm list of expectations and then upholding them is the key, according to Mr. Hodapp. He advised Mr. Cleveland to make a list of 10 expectations, those behaviors that Christy must do. For instance, school attendance and completing all homework would be reasonable expectations. Next to each of the expectations, Mr. Hodapp advised, write down the consequence for not meeting the expectation. Consequences should mostly consist of losing privileges and freedoms. Then sit the girl down and explain it all to her. After that, you just have to apply the rules consistently. Mr. Cleveland did exactly this because it seemed to be a logical and sound approach, but he wonders if there isn't more to dealing with his daughter than the dry rationality of enforcing rules.

Mr. Ellis Cleveland and his wife, Marjorie, separated 8 months before this latest school incident. Their separation has been very stressful and painful for the entire family. Christy is the Clevelands' only child. She lives with her father in a small midwestern town. Her mother lives in a large city an hour and 15 minutes away.

The Clevelands were wed on the day after their high school graduation, over 15 years ago. Ellis took a job at a muffler shop, and Marjorie worked part-time in the dining room of a nursing home. From the start, their relationship was fraught with difficulties. Alcohol abuse and marital infidelity on both sides made for a household of secrets, tension, and conflict.

During the first 9 years of the marriage, Ellis's only sober moments came during the workday. He proved himself to be an able auto mechanic and supervisor, gradually working himself up to shop manager. At home, however, he was frequently drunk, irritable, and verbally abusive to both Marjorie and Christy. It seemed that the more miserable he got, the more he drank, and the more he drank, the more miserable he got.

When Ellis's drinking habit expanded to his work site, his employees at the garage confronted him with his problem. He accompanied a coworker to an Alcoholics Anonymous meeting and started on his recovery. Despite an occasional slip, Ellis has been basically dry for the past 6 years.

Sobriety gave Ellis the sudden ability to see that his marriage was in shambles. He and his wife hardly knew each other. He soon discovered that Marjorie had gone through a string of boygriends while he had been passed out on the couch in front of the television. Ellis and Marjorie struggled, often arguing late into the night. Their words brought them no resolution; in fact, they only further amplified their feelings of anger and desperation. Marjorie admitted that she had been unfaithful in the past, but she contended that those days were long gone. Ellis wanted to believe her, but he suspected that she continued the affairs. He coped by devoting himself to his work and attending AA meetings almost every evening.

As an only child, Christy often enjoyed the full attention of one or both of her parents. Her father would take her on long hikes in the forest behind their house, hoisting her up on his shoulders to carry her when she tired on the way home. When he carried her, she felt like her father's special girl. Her mother was a talented amateur artist who patiently taught her daughter how to draw. The two spent lazy afternoons sketching rural landscapes filled with barns and covered bridges. While the love between her parents often was lacking, Christy developed very full and rewarding relationships with each of the two adults.

It would be inaccurate to claim that the difficulties between her parents did not confuse Christy. Her father often went on prolonged drinking binges. For weeks his mood would climb to an almost surreal ecstasy, as if he were the king of the world. Then, suddenly, he would dive into a deep depression. Christy learned to recognize the changes in the timbre and the tone of his voice and to know when her father was becoming agitated and unreasonable. She would lock herself in her room and hide under her bed while her father raged at her mother or shouted at the empty living room.

Also contributing to Christy's delicate sense of confusion was the inconsistency of her mother's love. Sometimes her mother was caring and emotionally available to Christy. Other times, she seemed far away, distant and unfeeling. At those moments, she would remain polite and casual but uninvolved, acting more like a temporary roommate than a loving mother. Also during these time, Christy's mother seemed to yearn for independence, for a way to be somewhere else, far from her troubled family. Occasionally, she would stay out all night. Christy would sleep on the couch and wait for her mother to come home. The next morning her mother would breeze in like a harried celebrity on a world tour. Offering no excuses for her absence and no apologies for her insensitivity, she would gather up a few things and rush off again.

Christy is an eighth-grade student at Abner Doubleday Junior High School. Until recently, she had always been a solid student, earning A's and B's in most of her subjects. Throughout the five elementary grades, her teachers generally found her to be agreeable and hard working. As a fifth grader, she won the highly competitive district science fair, defeating entrants from four elementary schools. Last year, when she went into the junior high school, Christy's attitude and effort began to change. The girl who was so proud of her school achievement seemed to avoid the limelight of success. Her grades fell to straight C's. When her father asked her why her grades had dropped, Christy shrugged and said, "I'm not into the honor roll anymore, Dad. That stuff's for little kids and nerds."

Christy's alienation from school and academic achievement was futher fueled by her parents' separation. Her parents gave her a week to choose which parent she wanted to live with. She found herself torn. While she leaned toward living with her father, she feared insulting and rejecting her mother. As the decision day arrived, Christy's mother suddenly declared that she didn't want Christy living with her. She had married too young and had never been on her own. This was her chance to be independent. Christy took this as a terrible rejection. She moved in with her father. She now visits her mother every other weekend.

CASE 24

TALK ISN'T CHEAP

THE INCIDENT

Ms. Lois Sampson, the creative writing teacher, is standing in front of the room lecturing to her students on the steps needed to edit their compositions. As she reads from her book, she directs students to turn to page 53 in their textbook to follow along as she reads. She begins by reading aloud, "It is essential that your completed composition be well edited."

Midway through the sentence, she hears a young voice cry out, "Yo, Keasha, look at this masterpiece." It is Vershon, who is talking to Keasha as he shows her his composition.

Keasha quickly scans the page. Upon seeing her name, she cries out, "Hey, what's my name doing on your paper?" Immediately, Ms. Sampson looks up from her book and glares at Keasha.

At the same time, Vershon whispers, "Girl, keep it quiet." Ms. Sampson finishes reading the sentence and then stops the class.

"Do I have to stop class again because someone is talking?" she announces to the class. In a chorus of muffled, sleepy voices the students say "No."

For Ms. Sampson, talking is the biggest problem that she is having with her students. Often when she is lecturing at the front of the room, half the students ignore her and talk among themselves. The situation so bad, in fact, that Mr. Kasaski, the principal, has had to pop in on a number of occasions to quiet the students' voices. In her most recent evaluation, Mr. Kasaski wrote, "It is critical that you work at better classroom management to control the volume level in your classes. This is a problem with serious ramifications." Along with this comment came a "low" rating on the evaluation form. In turn, this meant that she would not receive the large salary increase that she had hoped for, but instead would again receive low merit pay.

BACKGROUND INFORMATION

Lois is a second-year teacher at Quigley High School who struggled in her first year of teaching. It was only through the intervention of her mentor, Flo, that Lois was even hired back. Flo and Lois worked together last year to try to increase student interest and reduce off-task behaviors, such as talking and goofing around. Flo, herself in her third year, had frequently witnessed students talking out, out of their seats, and talking back to Lois during her observations. Lois had graduated in the top of her college class and received honors for her grade average, but upon graduating, her teaching was less than successful. This is evidenced by comments on her first-year evaluation: "Lois is extremely knowledgeable about techniques and strategies. Her 'book knowledge' is indicative of great potential." Indeed, Lois could name many different types of effective teaching and classroom management techniques; however, the techniques often failed because of her poor execution. Even Flo recognized the errors in her teaching, but was unable to help her remedy them. As Flo put it, "Lois is extremely intelligent, but when it comes to applying it, she is a million miles away."

Lois often uses nagging to get students to complete assignments and to remain quiet. Her threat of sending them to detention only goes so far. She realizes that many of the students whom she would send to detention either work or have to baby-sit their younger siblings after school. For these reasons alone many of her threats of detention go unfulfilled. On those rare occasions when she sends students to detention, they often sleep through it or end up getting sent home early by the detention teacher. And then there are those days, quite frequent, when students are sent home anyway because no one is available to supervise the detention room. Lois often blames the school's inconsistent use of detention ("I have no support") or poor parenting skills ("Parents just don't care") for inappropriate student behaviors in her class. "Their behavior is just beyond my control," she once said to Mr. Kasaski.

Quigley High School is not an easy place for a new teacher to perfect her skills. The urban setting repeatedly yields fights, drugs, and a less than secure environment for learning. As you enter Quigley, one of the first things that you notice is the noise level. The plaster walls and tall ceilings amplify voices and sounds. For many alumni, Quigley High School was a place of honor and tradition that carried many fond memories for them. Today, however, the walls are cracked, the books are old, and most of the faculty is new. Mr. Kasaski remembers those glory days and he tries to relate that feeling to his current students. But Mr. Kasaski also thinks that today's students represent an entirely new generation of kids that don't often use words like *pride, honor,* and *hard work* in their vocabulary.

Both Keasha and Vershon have been attending Quigley for the past two years. They live in the same neighborhood and have been classmates since childhood. Over the years, they have become good friends. In times of trouble, they have always been there for each other. For instance, a few years ago when Keasha's father came home drunk and began to hit her, it was Vershon who came to her rescue to push her father out of the house. Likewise, when Vershon lost his younger sister to a drug overdose, it was Keasha who was there to comfort him and to get him through the rough times. In high school, both students have excelled and plan to attend college upon graduation, making these two students sparkling rarities for Quigley. Over the past 10 years in his neighborhood, Vershon has witnessed beautiful homes with caring neighbors transform into crack houses with nightly police raids. But rather than fall into the trappings of the "big money" from dealing drugs, Vershon and Keasha have sought refuge in their local church to stay on the straight and narrow path. Keasha is active in the choir and Vershon works with young children in an after-school program.

Despite their talent and their fondness for Ms. Sampson, both students see creative writing class as a joke. They fail to see a relevant connection between creative writing and their career goals. Vershon, who wants to be a chef and restaurant owner, often complains that most of the academic "stuff" in school will not help him in his future. Similarly, Keasha, who wants to be a veterinarian, often does not complete writing assignments. She has told Ms. Sampson that she "hates" writing. Meanwhile, Ms. Sampson has very few curricular resources at her disposal for students and makes do with decade-old books and limited supplies of writing paper. Her class has access to two computers in the library, but the entire school must share them. Lacking ideas and old before her time, Ms. Sampson has considered quitting and working for a book publisher.

TATTLETALE

THE INCIDENT

"Quietly now! Quietly now!" Ms. Stanfield half-whispers and half-shouts to her fifth-grade class as they noisily fumble with their coats in the closet at the rear of the room. They have just come in from the playground. Mr. Lewis, the paraprofessional who monitors recess, enters with John. Mr. Lewis looks perplexed and tired. His right hand is set firmly on the student's shoulder, holding the youngster in place. John's head hangs low in embarrassment and he wiggles his shoulders in a half-hearted attempt to free himself from Mr. Lewis's grasp. The paraprofessional marches the youngster up to the teacher at the front of the room.

"Where have you been?" Ms. Stanfield asks John. He stares at his feet in silence.

"He did it again, Ms. Stanfield. This time I found him way out in the forest, a good two hundred yards off the playground. He was messing in the creek," explains Mr. Lewis.

Ms. Stanfield crouches down to John's level and speaks softly. "John, tell me why you ran off."

John keeps his eyes to the floor and mumbles one word. "Teasing."

"They were teasing you again?" asks the teacher. "Who was teasing you, John? You can tell me."

The boy's eyes well up with tears. He rubs his eyes and shakes his head.

"You won't tell me who teased you?" Ms. Stanfield queries. "If you tell me, I can help you."

John shakes his head vehemently. The other students in the class are now sitting at their desks. They have been watching with great interest.

BACKGROUND INFORMATION

John is a fifth-grade student who is extremely intelligent and very overweight. When he speaks, the words come out garbled and jumbled, sounding as if they had been mashed up and rearranged somewhere between his brain and his mouth. Although John tries to mask this speech impediment by speaking rarely or by whispering, his fellow students are aware of his pronunciation difficulties. He receives speech and language services from a specialist who pulls John out of his class for brief one-on-one sessions and also provides language development activities for all the students in the general education class. Most of the students find John to be somewhat odd, primarily due to his speech and enormous size but also because of his somewhat obsessive desire to talk about computers and adult books no one else has read.

John struggles to fit in with the other students during recess. He plays with different groups, never settling in long enough to become a regular. Some days he wanders around alone, circling the periphery of the playground, watching the other children from a distance. Recently he has tried to play with Wendell and Billy, two boys who climb on the giant rocks at the point where the playground meets the woods. They stand on top of the large stones and talk about space travel and science fiction movies. John shares these interests, but he also finds these boys to be somewhat childish when they play with their action figures and make goofy noises. The fact that Wendell and Billy tend to babble on endlessly is a source of both comfort and annoyance to John. He is able to be part of the little group without talking very often. Yet he is also too aware of his role as the third wheel on the bike, a vehicle only somewhat to his liking.

One reason John tends to hang around with Wendell and Billy has little to do with the two boys and their interests. It comes down to location. The big rocks are far away from any other group of children. Most importantly, they are at a great distance from the tough boys who often tease John because of his weight and his garbled speech.

When the tough boys first teased John, he immediately told Ms. Stanfield. She punished the boys who had called John names. For the rest of the week, those boys called John a tattletale. To John's surprise, many of the other children did, too. Suddenly the problem of being picked on by a few mean boys had exploded into an enormous situation. John was taunted by kids he didn't even know, including some ribbon-haired girls who he thought were nice to everyone. John learned very quickly that he had broken a code of the schoolyard. Only the weakest child could get away with running to the teacher and telling on somebody. Eveyone knew that being a tattletale was even worse than being fat or talking funny.

John decided never to tattle on his classmates again. For the next 2 months, he clung to Mr. Lewis's side as protection from the tough guys who called him names. Mr. Lewis allowed John to sit by him at recess for a few days, then he began to encourage John to play with his peers. At first, the encouragement came in gentle words. "Wouldn't you rather play ball with the other kids?" Mr. Lewis would say. "I'm just a boring old man who sits on a bench." After a while, Mr. Lewis became pretty impatient. He pushed John to socialize, ordering him firmly, "Go out there and play with the other children. You're not sitting with me. I'm not your nursemaid." John took the hint and starting playing with Billy and Wendell.

As Ms. Stanfield speaks to John about running away and the way the other children tease him, she is reminded of her discussion with John's parents just 1 week before. In that parent-teacher conference, Ms. Stanfield listened as John's parents, Jaime and Ed, expressed their concerns about John's difficulties making friends. They were worried about John becoming an outcast, a loner.

John is the youngest child in the family. His three sisters are all 10 or more years older. John was a bit of a surprise to Jaime and Ed, who had considered their childbearing years to be long over when they found out they had a fourth baby on the way. They welcomed the new addition, but they also found young John to be more of a challenge than their previous three children. Even as an infant, he often seemed dissatisfied, inexplicably sullen, and listless. He was diagnosed with a severe articulation disorder and began receiving speech therapy when he was 4 years old. He has made steady progress, yet he still has a long way to go if his speech is to be understood by more than his family. Additionally, despite his parent's best efforts to regulate his diet, John has inherited his father's weight problem, a burden that John's sisters somehow escaped.

"Sometimes I just don't know what to do with him," Jaime confessed to Ms. Stanfield, "There are days when he seems resigned to the fact that he won't make any friends. At least two days a week he cries and begs me to let him stay home from school."

Additionally, Ms. Stanfield knows that her class this year has not yet become a peaceful and unified group. She has struggled in dealing with a wide range of troubling social dynamics, primarily concerning two groups of students. The team of tough boys who tease John consists of an inner circle of two leaders, Matt and Cedric, and a continuously shifting lineup of three to six other boys who tend to follow the negative leadership of the central two. For the first 2 weeks of the year, Ms. Stanfield heard consistent reports from students that Matt and Cedric were terrorizing their peers in the boys' room and in the long hallway behind the gym. Then the reports suddenly stopped, but not because the intimidation had ended. It seemed more as if everyone had gotten the message not to tell the teacher. Ms. Stanfield has tried to win over the two lead boys by designating them as her special classroom helpers. The boys have obediently completed the various chores assigned to them, but that seems to have had no effect on the many subtle ways they intimidate their peers.

The second group of youngsters that concerns Ms. Stanfield consists of four girls, all hard workers and teacher-pleasers. Although all four do well in their academics, Ms. Stanfield is worried about the way the girls criticize their peers because of clothing and appearance. The girls are fortunate enough to own and wear expensive designer clothes and shoes to school. They have set a divisive, competitive standard for appearance in the room. At times, they have picked on John and others because of physical characteristics such as size and hair color. Ms. Stanfield has spoken to the girls about their behavior, but their preoccupation with appearance seems firmly entrenched.

CASE **26**

VALENTINE'S DAY

THE INCIDENT

As the fifth-period bell chimed through the halls of Dewey High School, Mr. Rollins searched inside his cluttered briefcase for his lecture notes and a well-worn Keats anthology. Hearing a shriek and a roar of laughter, he looked up to see a noisy huddle of students gathering at the back of his classroom.

"Just move your butt and gimme the seat," Torre demanded. Sylvia did not move. Her face was red with fear and embarrassment, and her eyes darted around as if looking for someone to save her from this menace. She turned to her friend, Elsa, who was sitting behind her. Elsa quickly supplied the necessary protection.

"Little Torre boy," Elsa jeered, "why don't you just sit up front with the rest of the hillside nerds?" The students in the back of the class laughed. Torre reached out and grabbed something from Elsa'a hands. She immediately lunged forward, sprawling across Sylvia's desk and clamping onto Torre's jacket.

Mr. Rollins rushed forward and nudged his way to the center of the commotion. Torre and Elsa were tangled on the floor in a wrestling match. Elsa had Torre in a headlock. Torre was curled up in a ball on the floor. He clutched a red envelope, a Valentine's Day card, to his chest. "That's mine! Give me it!" Elsa shouted as she grabbed for the paper. Torre's body shook with laughter at her feeble attempts to take the envelope away. Repeatedly Torre said, "Whore! Whore!" The more he repeated the insult, the harder Elsa tried to pull the card from his hands.

BACKGROUND INFORMATION

Dewey High School is situated at the edge of an old working-class neighborhood. The students are predominantly white. About half live in the local neighborhood. The rest ride buses from newer, more affluent areas that are building up in the surrounding hills. In the past decade, the composition of Dewey High has changed dramatically, due to the influx of middle-class students. The growth of middle-class housing is the result of the sudden inundation of computer software and engineering companies across the hilly outskirts of town. Shiny new office parks sprang up almost overnight. The hill region was quickly developed into posh housing complexes—with gates and security guards—and new shopping areas consisting of stylish, upscale shops and restaurants.

There are tensions in town and in the high school, a general strain between the old blue-collar families and the new professional class. At Dewey High School, the working-class students are known as "townies" and the more affluent students are called "hillsiders." Some of the townies feel that their old mill town is being stolen away and modernized by outsiders who don't really care. Some hillsiders look down at the townies because of their coarse styles of dress and unrefined modes of behavior.

Mr. Rollins is a first-year English teacher at Dewey High School. While some of his colleagues grumble about the vulgar manners and language of "this younger generation," Mr. Rollins finds himself fascinated with the creativity and spirit of the adolescents he teaches. He has received some criticism from colleagues for his tendency to run a loose, wide-open classroom—that is, for allowing students too much freedom. He runs a relaxed, conversational classroom that encourages student participation. He feels comfortable with students talking out without raising hands, and he doesn't mind the students' occasionally suggestive language. Still, as a new teacher, he realizes that he needs to maintain a positive image among his professional peers. He knows this may require structuring his classes in a more traditional and fixed way.

Elsa Thompson is a 15-year-old "townie" who lives with her father and two younger sisters in an old frame house half a mile from the high school. Her parents divorced when Elsa was 11. Her father was recently laid off when the glass plant closed. He had worked at the plant for 26 years. In order to make ends meet, he now works at the hardware store during the day and moonlights as a security guard for a well-to-do hillside housing development in the evening. Elsa misses him and worries about her younger sisters, ages 7 and 9. Lacking a parental figure around the house, Elsa ends up filling in as a sort of stand-in mom. For instance, she is responsible for getting her two sisters up and off to school in the morning. She prepares breakfast, makes sure the girls are properly dressed, and walks them to the bus stop at the end of the road. These responsibilities sometimes make Elsa late for her own school day.

Elsa is a very capable English student who enjoys Mr. Rollins's class. The hallway gossips at Dewey have her pegged as a sexually promiscuous girl who too quickly leaps from one boyfriend to another. Mr. Rollins has noticed that she is often flirtatious, but he has quietly questioned the accuracy of her loose reputation. He knows that one can never know the truthfulness of rumors. He is also aware of the inequity of the sexual rumor mill, that the status of "having a reputation" is easily branded on girls and rarely on boys. He has recently noticed how frequently demeaning terms for girls and women, terms such as *whore* and *bitch,* have become commonplace in the students' hallway dialogues.

Elsa prides herself on her independence and toughness. She can match wits and trade insults with any of the boys. She dresses in a rugged style, jeans and black leather jackets. There are times when Mr. Rollins wonders whether certain boys are trying to intimidate or harass Elsa. More than once he has observed her in the school parking lot after school, smoking cigarettes and arguing with tough-looking boys. She seems to handle herself very well in difficult situations. Mr. Rollins still wonders why she puts herself in such combative situations. He also fears that there may be other, more vicious encounters in which Elsa is not able to hold her own.

Torre Fuscetta is a "hillsider." His family moved to town 2 years ago, when his father took a sales director position with a local software company. Torre enjoys being a member of the wrestling team and often wears his Dewey letter jacket to class. Although apparently an able English student, his effort in Mr. Rollins's class has been inconsistent. Mr. Rollins has consulted with Torre's other teachers and found that he tries much harder in his other subjects. When Mr. Rollins jokingly presented this fact to Torre and asked what he could do to stir the student's interest in English, Torre responded, "If you'd get rid of all the poetry and literature and writing assignments, this would be an okay class." He seems to have only a minor interest in English.

On the other hand, Torre has demonstrated great interest in Elsa. Two weeks ago, Mr. Rollins found Elsa and Torre nestled together seductively under the back stairway. He quickly rousted them and advised them to place limits on the publicly physical nature of their budding romance. In the past week, however, some of Mr. Rollins's students informed him that Elsa had jilted Torre in favor of one of the guys on the basketball team. Elsa switched her usual seat in English class to a spot far away from her ex-boyfriend. Torre did not take the rejection easily. He changed his seat also, following Elsa, shooting her angry glances when he thought the teacher wasn't looking. Elsa again changed her seat. Torre again changed his seat in response.

This shifting and reshifting of seats has become a daily hassle as Elsa moves to get away and Torre follows in a mocking, tormenting style. Mr. Rollins does not like to assign seats to his students. He likes the students to make decisions about where to sit and how to participate. But he is losing patience with this game of musical chairs and beginning to see no other alternative. As the conflict between Elsa and Torre is obvious to all in the class, Mr. Rollins is considering a class discussion about the problem. Perhaps that would move them toward a solution. He hesitates to initiate such a conversation, though, for fear that the topic of discussion will be unduly embarrassing to Elsa or Torre. He figures that dating relationships and sexuality might be very difficult topics for this group of teenagers to discuss openly.

On the afternoon of the wrestling match, Elsa had arranged for three of her friends to save her a single seat in the corner of the classroom. Her three friends filled the adjoining seats, thereby making it impossible for Torre to sit next to Elsa. Torre badgered one of these friends, Sylvia, to give up her seat to him. Because she refused to move, Torre reached for a red envelope jutting out of Elsa's notebook. He grabbed the Valentine's Day card that Elsa had purchased for her new boyfriend. Elsa leaped forward to retrieve the card, resulting in the fracas and Mr. Rollins's intervention.

CASE **27**

SOFT-SPOKEN

 THE INCIDENT

Most of the small group of high school boys have started working on their individual mathematics assignments. Ms. Rojas peers from her desk at the front of the room to the back row and notices that neither Norm nor Rico have opened their books. Norm is tilting back nonchalantly in his seat and humming a song under his breath. He is tapping the desk lightly, using his fingers as drumsticks. Rico is bent over as if working on the math problems, but he is grinning and his eyes are fixed on Norm. Ms. Rojas says: "Now is the time to work on your assignments. If you don't work, you won't earn your points toward Friday's pizza party."

"I got your points, bi-," Norm mumbles in a voice barely audible to the teacher.

Ms. Rojas is startled. Adrenaline quickly rushes through her body. Her first impression is that Norm just called her "bitch," but she can't be sure. He's never spoken to her in that way in the past. "Excuse me, Norm, did you say something?" Ms. Rojas asks in a puzzled tone.

"No problem here, teacher," Norm states clearly, then his voice trails off, ". . . stu- . . . bit-." These final words are again ambiguous to Ms. Rojas. She feels her face flush with heat. From Norm's mumbled words, she heard him call her a "stupid bitch." Or at least she thinks he did. She wonders if he is baiting or taunting her. But it seems out of character for him.

Whatever Norm said, it is very clear to the students sitting near him. Student eyes from the desks near Norm stare wide open with intrigue, tracking first to Norm and then to Ms. Rojas at her desk. Pencils have stopped scratching out mathematics problems. The class is silent and tense. Ms. Rojas watches Norm closely. His head is down, so she can only see the top of his head and the collar of his winter coat pulled up tall around his ears. She looks over at Rico. His body and head are in a similar posture, as if he were looking for something he had lost on the floor beneath his desk.

Finally, after 5 seconds of heavy silence, Rico can't stand it. "Oh man!" he exclaims. He quickly presses his hand over his mouth to hush his own nervous laughter.

Ms. Rojas stands up and walks in front of her desk. Her eyes meet Norm's as each wonders what the other will do next.

BACKGROUND INFORMATION

This scene takes place in a self-contained special education class for students considered to have emotional/behavioral disorders (E/BD). The class is located in the vocational wing of Dwight Evans High School. Ms. Rojas works with 10 high school students in this special program.

Dwight Evans High School serves 710 students in a medium-sized, rural town in the Pacific Northwest that has gone through a surprising amount of change in recent years. Traditionally, the surrounding valley region has been filled with family dairy farms and apple orchards. Many fathers and mothers in the area either owned farms or worked in the large apple and dairy processing industries. Additionally, many parents of students at Evans High worked in nearby rubber and plastic products factories. In the past 5 years, however, the rubber and plastics plants have closed down as those jobs have been sent overseas. More than 50% of the family farmers have sold out to large, international agribusiness corporations.

These economic changes have been unsettling to numerous families in the community. Many parents, including Rico's father, lost their good-paying factory jobs. Although Rico's father now works two part-time retail jobs and does house-painting on the side, he brings home barely half of what he used to earn in the factory.

The local schools have struggled economically as the tax base in the county has dropped. As the unemployment rate rose and good jobs became harder to come by, the housing values fell. The school district is primarily funded by home property taxes, so the fall in housing values led to a decrease in funds for the schools. In each of the past 3 years, the local school district has attempted to pass along part of its financial woes to school employees by elevating the amount that teachers and other staff have to pay for health insurance. Many of the best teachers have been seeking jobs in surrounding districts where the pay and benefits are somewhat higher. Other positions (such as teacher's aide slots) have been left unfilled to save dollars. Overall, the morale of the teachers and staff is not good. There is an effort under way to unionize the teachers and staff in order to fight for higher wages and benefits.

The teacher morale issues have been compounded by the poor performance of the Evans High students on the most recent round of state achievement tests. Following the federal No Child Left Behind Act, this state's Department of Education has instituted a vigorous testing and accountability program. Schools that fare poorly on the annual achievement test batteries are put on probationary status and given one year to bring up the school's test scores. The school principal, Dr. Goldfarb, and the teachers have had numerous meetings to learn about the state tests and how to prepare their students. The principal and the teachers feel a great amount of pressure.

Ms. Rojas was the only new teacher hired at Evans High this year. Her students receive all of their instruction in all of their subjects from this one teacher in this one classroom. Next door to her room is a similar class instructed by Mr. Toulouse, a 10-year veteran who has been very active in the unionization activities. Both classrooms are supposed to have a teacher's aide, but neither position has been filled in recent years.

In the past, Dr. Goldfarb was pretty quick to give students in the E/BD programs out-of-school suspensions for substantial violations of school rules. Despite the strict limitations and procedural requirements in the Individuals with Disabilities Education Act, Dr. Goldfarb often suspended these students. This year, though, with the pressure on to bring up test scores, Dr. Goldfarb does not want any students to miss academic time. So he has been very hesitant to use out-of-school suspension as a punishment. He has created an Alternative Consequences Committee, which is made up of five veteran teachers from different academic departments and one school guidance counselor. The committee comes up with alternatives to suspension in an attempt to reduce the out-of-school time of students who have violated school rules. For example, some violators have spent Saturday mornings or Tuesday evenings working to clean and beautify the school grounds. The Evans faculty is split on whether this new committee is effective and innovative or, as some teachers say, "soft on crime."

The students in the two E/BD classrooms spend some time together during the school week, but they have no interactions with the general population of Dwight Evans High School. The two classes eat lunch together in the empty cafeteria after all of the other Evans students have finished eating and moved on to their afternoon classes. The two classes attend art, music, and physical education classes once per week as a combined group.

Ms. Rojas's class has been relatively calm and stable in recent weeks, a far cry from the daily battle of wills that took place from September through November. When she first arrived in the fall, she found that many of her students maintained a great allegiance to their previous teacher. During those first few weeks, it seemed that no matter what Ms. Rojas did, some student would complain that "Miss Anderson never did it that way." The students were often rebellious and noncompliant. Ms. Rojas tried to be patient with them. She knew that six of the students had been in Ms. Anderson's class for three straight years. These tough, hard-talking boys had come to trust and rely on Ms. Anderson. Ms. Rojas knew that it would take time for the students to do the same with her. Gradually, the students began to accept Ms. Rojas as their teacher. By Christmas, Ms. Rojas could rightly claim that she had become the teacher of the class.

Ms. Rojas uses the point/level system of behavior management that was given to her by Mr. Toulouse. Students can earn 1 point per half hour for each of the following general behavior categories: following directions; staying on task; using good language; keeping hands and feet to self. Students who tally above 80% of the total possible points on a given day are given a star next to their name on the big wall chart. A student who earns 15 stars moves up to the next level. For major rule infractions such as hitting a peer or leaving an assigned area, students automatically lose an entire level. The system has 4 levels. Students start at the beginning of the first level and, hopefully, work their way up to level 4 during the year. A student who moves up the levels is given more privileges and fun activities. In addition, Ms. Rojas and Mr. Toulouse occasionally plan a special Friday afternoon activity such as a pizza party or a movie. Individual students must get over 80% of their points for the entire week to participate. Those who earn the necessary points go to Ms. Rojas' room for fun activities while the rest go to Mr. Toulouse's room for quiet seatwork time. The two teachers trade off their own Friday afternoon roles, entertainment manager and taskmaster, each week.

Norm Ferguson is the only student still on the first level. The other students are scattered evenly across levels 2, 3, and 4. Twice Norm has earned his way up to level 2 only to drop back to level 1 for a major rule infraction, walking out of the classoom without permission. Both times Norm had become very angry at a peer, and his way of avoiding a possible physical confrontation or blowing his top was to quickly run out of the room. After his second major rule infraction and required level drop, Norm lost all enthusiasm for earning points and climbing the levels.

Ms. Rojas has just started to wonder if the points/levels system is helping her students. Three of her students are highly motivated by the rewards. Another four are only motivated occasionally by the system. They seem to pay attention only when they are already very close to earning a reward. The other three students hardly pay any attention to the points, levels, and rewards. Additionally, Ms. Rojas wonders if teenagers should be trying to earn pizza, time on the computer, and sodas. She wonders how this is preparing them for the world beyond her little room, a world where they will soon be expected to find jobs, pay rent, and behave as adults.

Of all her students, only Norm was never in Ms. Anderson's class. Unlike the others who had been labeled BD and educated in special programs for most of their school career, Norm had been placed in Ms. Rojas' class only 3 months prior to the incident.

During the spring of the prior year, two major changes occurred in Norm's life. His parents separated after 22 years of marriage. Norm remained with his mother in the family home while his father moved across town. Soon thereafter, Norm was thrown out of Thorndike School, a local private academy. He had tapped into the school computer system, accessed the hall locker combinations, and proceeded to steal more than $2,000 worth of his peers' personal belongings. When he was finally caught, he attempted suicide with sleeping pills. He spent the summer receiving treatment in a private psychiatric hospital.

As a tenth-grader, Norm had never attended public school. Because of his expulsion from Thorndike, other private schools in the area declined him admission. He entered Evans High School in September. By November, he had been suspended 3 times for fighting and verbally threatening other students. A number of his teachers told the principal that they and many of the students feared Norm. They referred him for evaluation and possible placement in special education. Despite the fact that Norm's disciplinary record at Thorndike had been spotless, the evaluation committee decided that his recent violent behavior was serious enough to warrant the BD label and placement in Ms. Rojas's class.

Ms. Rojas found Norm to be a very angry, brooding figure who often seemed overwhelmed by the power of his own emotions. He had a soft-spoken and kind manner of interaction, yet his words often seemed tinged with bitterness and irony. Ms. Rojas and the school guidance counselor led group counseling sessions with the boys 2 afternoons per week. It was evident in these sessions that Norm did not like to discuss himself or his family, preferring to keep his problems to himself. He seemed to hold his fiery anger within his tense shoulders and deeply furrowed brow. Ms. Rojas found that humor was the best way to work with Norm. She teased him sometimes about being so private with his troubles. He enjoyed the teasing and joking.

"Don't you go telling anybody that you're mad or anything, Norm," she'd joke. "Wouldn't want to let anybody know you're human."

Norm would chuckle and come right back at her. "That's 'cause I'm not human, Miz R. I'm a robot sent down by evil aliens. I'm programmed to haunt you for the rest of your days."

Ms. Rojas would laugh and sneak up to whisper in his ear, "My pleasure."

Through this humorous connection, Ms. Rojas and Norm have been able to work well together. He had no major behavior difficulties in her class prior to the incident related here.

Ms. Rojas's primary worry about Norm is his academics. He completed a very intensive program of ninth-grade study in a highly selective private school. His tenth-grade curriculum is supposed to include advanced courses in trigonometry, chemistry, world history, and European literature. Most of Ms. Rojas's students work three or four grade levels behind, and she has felt pretty able to handle that. But Norm's work is at such an advanced level that she hasn't felt prepared to meet his academic needs.

When Ms. Rojas spoke to her supervisor, Dr. Goldfarb, the principal of Dwight Evans High School, he told her to consult with the faculty in each of the appropriate academic areas to get assistance. She contacted the department chairs in math, physical science, history, and literature. The math and physical science chairs handed her copies of the tenth-grade curriculum standards and the teacher's versions of the texts. The literature department chair gave her a reading list of more than 50 novels and plays. He told her to contact him if she had any questions. The history chair had never responded to her multiple phone calls or e-mails. Ms. Rojas doesn't know what to do. She feels guilty each day when she gives Norm assignments in his subject areas and she often can't fully understand the work herself.

Ms. Rojas feels better able to provide for Rico Pena's academic needs. His first language is Spanish, and his family speaks very little English in their home. In academic testing, he understandably tends to score a grade or two low in English reading and writing skills. In mathematics, however, his skills are excellent. He scores at the top of his grade level in both mathematics reasoning and calculations.

Rico is the student who had the greatest emotional attachment to Ms. Anderson. Long after his classmates had warmed up to Ms. Rojas, he occasionally spent a day obsessing over his old teacher's absence. On those days, he would tell Ms. Rojas that she wasn't his real teacher. She could never take Ms. Anderson's place. Ms. Rojas would try to reassure Rico that she had no intention of taking Ms. Anderson's place in the students' hearts and minds but that she was the one and only teacher in this classroom.

Rico tends to be somewhat of an outcast in the class. It isn't that his peers completely dislike him. It is more that they tend not to notice him at all, as if he were invisible. He has no close friendships. Occasionally, he has latched on to a specific peer, becoming very dependent on that single boy. In recent weeks, Ms. Rojas has watched Rico follow Norm around the classroom. When the students went to lunch or took a break and played cards, Rico insisted on sitting next to Norm. At first, Norm seemed upset by all this attention. Then he seemed to like and take advantage of the attention. He had Rico do favors for him, run errands, clean up his locker, and keep his school supplies stocked. Ms. Rojas had wondered if she should talk to one or both of the boys, for it appeared to her that Norm was using Rico. She wasn't sure how either boy would react to such a confrontation.

Adding more fuel to the fire, Ms. Rojas was aware that the other boys in the class had been passing around stories about Rico and Norm being gay lovers. She had no idea if there was any truth to this, but she was concerned that the entire stew would soon reach a boil and blow the lid off the pot.

CASE **28**

Turning Upside-Down

The Incident

The youngsters in Ms. Grogan's second-grade class quickly place their jackets and personal items in the closet, sit down quietly at their desks, and begin the day with individual seatwork activities. Chris is an academically able child who has no difficulty handling the set of mathematics review sheets. But he is very active. He squirms about in his seat and knocks his papers and pencil to the floor.

"Chris," Ms. Grogan calls across the room in a soft voice.

"Yeah?" Chris asks innocently.

"You know."

"Yeah."

As Chris leans over to pick up the fallen items, he spins sideways in his seat like an acrobat, turning the small clean-up task into a prolonged gymnastic exercise. After he has replaced his pencil and papers on his desk, he sticks the pencil in his mouth and stares up at the ceiling. He seems to be daydreaming. He chews the pencil eraser with his teeth and spins the pencil with his hand. He accidentally drops the pencil to the floor. In an effort to retrieve the pencil, he sprawls on his stomach, lying across his chair with arms and legs balanced delicately in each direction. Ms. Grogan walks over to his desk and gently directs him to start his work. He finally retrieves his pencil and starts on an arithmetic problem.

After finishing the first of three math sheets, Chris spins his little body upside-down into a headstand. His rear end sticks upward, his feet dangle onto his desk, and his head is far below on the chair itself. Ms. Grogan verbally directs Chris to sit up straight, but he does not respond. Many of the other students are becoming distracted by Chris's acrobatics. They are off-task and giggling.

Background Information

This is not the first time that Chris has squirmed in his seat, dropped items on the floor, and flipped himself upside-down. It seems to Ms. Grogan that Chris goes through streaks of good and bad behavior that last for about 2 to 3 weeks. He would sit calm and upright in his seat for a few weeks, completing all of his academic work.

Then, for reasons unknown to Ms. Grogan, he would become increasingly antsy. His entire body would be restless and fidgety. During these squirmy days, he would push the seat away and work standing up. He appeared uncomfortable in his own body. The zenith of this hyperactivity occurred when Chris would stand on his head.

Ms. Grogan tried a number of interventions to help Chris sit quietly at his seat. Most often, she simply provided verbal redirection, telling Chris to sit appropriately at his desk. This seemed to have varied effectiveness. Sometimes Chris listened and corrected himself. Sometimes he seemed to be oblivious to her directions, behaving as if he didn't hear her or it didn't matter to him. When he did not respond to repeated verbal redirection, Ms. Grogan sent him to the time-out chair in the corner of the classroom. Typically, Ms. Grogan would end up telling Chris to go to time-out 3 or 4 times before he would respond. At times, he would stomp off angrily and sulk in the corner. Some days, he seemed to be in a sort of haze. He would stroll over to time-out wearing a dull, emotionless look on his face. Based on Ms. Grogan's records, the use of time-out has not reduced the frequency of Chris's headstands.

Ms. Grogan has recently started to wonder if her best bet isn't simply to put up with Chris's behavior and wait for the good, calm weeks to return. She is also aware that Chris's behavior often (not always) improves as the school day goes on. The initial moments of the morning seem to be the most hyperactive and disorganized for him, for some reason.

Ms. Grogan is a veteran teacher in her twenty-sixth year at Souther Elementary School. She has watched the student population of her school change dramatically over the years. As the local housing values have dropped within the city limits, the surrounding urban neighborhoods have shifted from White, middle-class home-owners to a predominantly working-class, ethnically diverse group of families. Many of the White families have moved to the new suburbs that have boomed to the west of the city. The urban neighborhoods that were once populated with first- and second-generation German, Italian, and Polish immigrants are now home to working poor families, mostly African Americans and Latin Americans.

Ms. Grogan has often commented to friends and colleagues that today's youngsters are entering school without the necessary level of social skills and language development. The new teachers tend to disagree with her, telling her that the students do not lack skills. They simply have their own style, their own ways of talking and interacting with others. They have encouraged Ms. Grogan to adapt, to become more in tune to her students' cultural backgrounds. Ms. Grogan is skeptical about these ideas. Although she still enjoys the creativity and spirit of her students, she believes them to be too often lacking in a sense of respect for her authority. She wonders what is happening to this new generation, why they can't be more orderly and proper as children used to be.

Ms. Grogan operates a very orderly yet friendly classroom. The walls are decorated with student art projects and writing samples, Halloween jack-o'-lanterns and ghosts on one bulletin board and student creative writing about what it would feel like to be an insect on the other. Her curriculum is a mix of the traditional and the latest approaches. Students meet in ability-level reading groups and use basal readers. She supplements these activities with phonics lessons and children's literature.

The daily schedule in Ms. Grogan class involves a gradual transition from quiet, individual work in the early morning to more social, cooperative group activities in the later morning and afternoon. Ms. Grogan believes that children need structure and silence in the morning to help them make the transition from the home environment to the demands of the school setting. She believes that once students settle in and become acclimated, then the activities can become more interactive and cooperative. Although Ms. Grogan has a reputation in her school for running a very tight ship, she is also viewed as being a fairly caring and even empathetic teacher.

Chris was transferred into Ms. Grogan's class in late September after he had a number of behavioral difficulties in another second-grade class. Not only had Chris squirmed and turned upside-down in that class, but when his teacher sent him to the office for refusing to sit upright, he called her a "bubble head" and raced out of the room. He ran out the back door of the school and lingered behind a tree at the far edge of the playground. The school principal and guidance counselor tried to first coax and then order him to return to the school building. Chris ran into the woods. He was later found playing with a dog behind a house in a nearby neighborhood.

That runaway incident spurred the principal to refer Chris for possible placement in a special education program for students with behavior disorders. The shift to Ms. Grogan's second-grade class was suggested by the guidance counselor, who sought to find an alternative means of dealing with Chris's behavior problems.

Chris's grandfather and guardian, Mr. Stewart, fully supported the class placement change to Ms. Grogan's room as an alternative to the behavior disorders classroom. He claimed that Chris was basically a good kid who had reacted emotionally to a number of difficulties in his life. From birth to age $4\frac{1}{2}$, Chris lived with his mother and father. His father worked as a roofer, and sometimes he drove an 18-wheeler on long hauls that took him away for weeks at a time. His mother worked as a nurse's aide in the evenings at a nursing home.

It is difficult to say exactly when alcohol and heroin started to dominate the lives of Chris's parents—and, therefore, Chris's life, too. They had always been big partyers, drinkers really, from the day they met in a beach bar on the west coast of Florida. Then his mother and one of the other nurse's aides started stealing prescription medications from the nursing home, and they would party with beer and the medications after a long night of work. Gradually, this became an almost daily pattern. While Chris was eating his breakfast with his father or his grandparents in the morning, his mother would stumble in the door, her feet dragging and her mouth moving a mile a minute. Soon thereafter Chris's dad started taking more and more long-haul jobs, keeping him away for longer periods of time.

When his father was home, Chris's parents argued and fought. As his mother became increasingly involved in alcohol and drugs, Chris's father would holler that she was ruining the family, that she had to stop. His mother lost her job at the nursing home, reducing the family to one income. And her supply of medications was no longer free. The few dollars that Chris's parents earned were flowing quickly into supporting his mother's addictions. The family moved from apartment to apartment on an almost monthly basis, skipping out on rent and utility payments, dodging creditors who called or came to the door. During the daytime, when Chris's mother wasn't sleeping, she was hanging out drinking with friends. Finally, after one long-haul job, Chris's father just didn't come back. He left the family once and for all.

Chris's mother often left him alone and unsupervised. The youngster found himself left in unknown places for hours and even days, entrusted to the uncertain care of acquaintances or even complete strangers.

One day a neighbor found 4-year-old Chris alone, crying in the corner of an apartment complex laundromat, and called the state Division of Youth and Family Services. After an investigation, his mother was ordered by the family court to enter a drug rehabilitation program. She asked her father, Chris's grand-father, to take care of Chris while she entered treatment for 90 days. Otherwise, Chris would enter the foster care system. The grandfather agreed only under the condition that she sign over permanent custody of the boy. Mr. Stewart had watched the maltreatment of young Chris for too long. He was determined to provide a permanent, stable home. At $4\frac{1}{2}$ years of age, Chris moved in with his grandfather, who cares for him to this day. Mr. Stewart is a 58-year-old middle school janitor who believes that a combination of strict discipline and love make for a proper, Christian upbringing. He has worked closely with the professionals at Souther Elementary to find a way for Chris to succeed.

Chris's mother currently lives in a small house 3 blocks away from Chris. He sees her on an irregular basis. She doesn't have a job. She is still very involved with drugs. The expense of the drugs has been great, so she has taken to doing small delivery jobs for one of the local street dealers. The family court sets offi-cial visiting times when she is supposed to spend time with Chris. She usually doesn't show up, although that doesn't stop Chris from hoping every time that she will. Sometimes, out of nowhere, she shows up at her father's house wearing a nice, clean dress and her hair up in a ribbon. Almost as if she were pretending that there was nothing wrong at all, or as if things were just about to get better for her and her son, she then spends an afternoon playing with and caring for Chris. For that short time, mother and son seem to erase all memory of what their lives together have really been like. They just enjoy the afternoon, maybe riding bikes or throwing a baseball. Then she leaves before the sun has gone down, and she is gone for weeks and weeks on end.

In a meeting with the guidance counselor, Chris admitted that he is better off living with his grandfather, but he hopes someday that he can live with his mom. He said the reason that he cannot live with her now is because she has a disease called alcoholism that makes her do the wrong things. He says that he, too, tends to do the wrong things. He says that he doesn't know why.

The guidance counselor asked him to draw a picture of himself. This is a fairly common projective technique that offers the counselor some insight into how a child thinks and feels about himself. Also, the picture can give the child and the counselor an entrée to talking about these thoughts and feelings, a door into a very frank discussion about self. When asked to draw a picture of himself, Chris drew a blue and red crayon boy with a straight, horizontal line for a mouth and an enor-mous heart that filled the entire torso. The heart was drawn upside-down.

CASE **29**

ALL WET

THE INCIDENT

Ms. Dodd, the director of Rhodes School, heard a child's shrieking voice echoing down the hallway. She stepped out of her office to see 4-year-old Edna running out of her classroom. The red-faced youngster was crying and panting in a flurry of anxiety. Her teacher, Ms. Springfield, chased close at Edna's heels. The director and the teacher converged on the screaming child, each adult kneeling and placing consoling hands on Edna's back and shoulders.

"There now, Edna, calm yourself down. We've got you. Everything is going to be all right," said Ms. Dodd in a soft, comforting tone. Little Edna buried her face in the director's shoulder and cried. Ms. Dodd cast a glance up at Ms. Springfield and whispered, "What happened?"

"It was Kyle Ehlenbeck," Ms. Springfield explained. "He peed on her foot."

"In the classroom?" Ms. Dodd asked with an air of mild surprise.

"Yes. I was lining them up to go to lunch and Edna and Kyle were missing. The kids were noisy, you know, all stirred up because of the trip to the zoo this afternoon. Kyle was teasing Edna, his ugly way of saying he likes her. He's been doing that quite a bit lately. I told him to stop. He did. Then the two of them went over to the corner and started fooling around behind the wall of bean bags. I knew Kyle was giving her a hard time, grabbing at her ponytail, but I was trying to give her a chance to stand up for herself. I guess I was wrong." Ms. Springfield felt guilty.

"These things are going to happen," Ms. Dodd reassured her teacher.

"I looked away for a moment. Edna screamed and ran out. Her sock and shoe are all wet. I came after Edna and Mr. Desco has Kyle." Ms. Springfield lifted Edna's foot and removed her wet shoe and sock.

"Do you have any idea why Kyle did this?"

Ms. Springfield shrugged her shoulders. "Hard to say, exactly. He's been having a hard week. He seems like he's upset all the time."

By this point, Edna had become silent. Her tears had stopped and her eyes were closed as if a short nap might make everything feel better. Ms. Dodd passed the sleepy-sad girl to her teacher and stood up. "Take care of Edna and send Kyle up to my office. First, I'll talk to Kyle, then I'll call his father in to discuss this."

Background Information

Rhodes School is located in a middle-class suburb of a large city. The school consists of three preschool classrooms, three kindergarten rooms, and a small day care center for infants. The program at Rhodes is based on Maria Montessori's principles of early learning and development. The program is holistic and integrated in nature, emphasizing the development of social cooperation, group solidarity, independence, creativity, and students' self-knowledge.

Ms. Springfield and Mr. Desco, the classroom aide, view themselves as gentle facilitators of child development and community activities, gently nudging and guiding children in explorations and discoveries about self and others. Their classroom is loosely structured, allowing the children many opportunities for choice in learning and play activities. The students generally get along well together. When conflicts between the youngsters do arise, neither Ms. Springfield or Mr. Desco have much patience. They tend to become anxious and hurriedly separate children when they start to squabble. Ms. Dodd has talked to Ms. Springfield about intervening more slowly, thereby allowing the children more of a chance to work things out for themselves. Ms. Springfield understands that children need to learn to work out social disagreements, but she also feels that her teacher role requires her to run a peaceful, orderly group lacking disagreements and fights.

Ms. Dodd believes that discipline is a prerequisite condition for learning. She is schooled in the Montessori belief that discipline is really an "inner discipline," and that children develop discipline from their own behavior and in conjunction with their home. As they learn and grow, they also develop self-discipline (or self-control) along the way. According to Ms. Dodd, "undisciplined children" are children who are really frustrated by the lack of proper stimulation and an inadequate opportunity to achieve.

Ms. Springfield and Mr. Desco lead a class of 4- and 5-year-old youngsters. Their classroom is very busy. It is filled with colorful objects, most created by the students. Enormous box-kite mobiles that look like birds and airplanes hang from the high ceiling. The floor has a scattering of small, multicolored rugs that seem to wander about the room, shifting place almost constantly. Child-size beanbags and pillows are piled up in one corner of the room. Books, hand puppets, building blocks, musical instruments, and toys line the shelves along one wall of the room. The adjacent wall is comprised of small cubbyholes where the children place their personal items. Coats hang on hooks above the cubbies. Ms. Springfield and Mr. Desco share a large desk positioned like an island in the very center of the room.

Although this is the first incident in which Kyle has urinated on a peer, this is only one of a series of troubling acts of misbehavior committed by the boy in the past 3 weeks. His mood has been one of barely concealed anger that bursts forth in occasional tussles with peers over toys or a place in line. These conflicts have gotten pretty physical. Kyle has hit or bitten a classmate 5 times over the past 2 weeks. Each time it seemed to Ms. Springfield that Kyle lashed out with little provocation. On previous occasions, Ms. Springfield used traditional Montessori discipline techniques. However, on 2 of these occasions, Ms. Springfield felt that Kyle's violent behavior was concern enough to warrant a trip to the office and a call to Mr. Ehlenbeck, Kyle's father.

Ms. Springfield and Mr. Desco mostly handle discipline problems in the traditional Montossori way. For example, positive classroom rules are listed on the board and followed by both the teacher and students. Moreover, these rules are reviewed daily and when a child does break a rule, he or she is reminded of the positive rule. Both adults in the class typically model the rules for the children and then verbalize which rule they just modeled. Ms. Springfield and Mr. Desco believe that they need to keep the children busy in meaningful activities, thereby preventing discipline problems. In doing so, the children are focused on positive activities and there is a reduced need for negative behaviors. Should a student behave inappropriately, the teacher reviews the positive rule, models the rule for the child, and then allows the child to exhibit the positive rule or behavior. For Kyle this has happened a few times. More recently, when he began to throw blocks at other children, Ms. Springfield demonstrated how to stack the blocks. When Kyle continued to throw them, she explained why it was important to care for the blocks and explained that if he continued to throw them, he would not be allowed to use them. Despite her best efforts, Kyle still threw the blocks. Because of his inappropriate use and care for the blocks, Kyle was not permitted to play with them again until he could tell his teacher that he would use them properly. He threw blocks several times in the past 2 weeks, despite his promise to "play nice."

Another technique that Ms. Springfield uses is the "quiet chair." The quiet chair is used when children are unable to maintain inner control. It has been used by a number of children, but Kyle seems to be the most frequent chair visitor. Children in her class who scream or are disruptive are sent to the quiet chair to reflect on their behavior and regain their composure. A recent incident illustrates how it was used with Kyle. Two days ago Ms. Springfield caught Kyle throwing blocks. She told him, "Throwing blocks at other children is not okay. Sit in this chair and get control." After Kyle was able to gain self-control, he was asked to return to play with the child whom he hit with blocks. As he was playing, Mrs. Springfield repeated the positive rule that he was exhibiting.

In other cases, when it was time to clean up, Kyle has had to repeatedly pick up blocks that he has knocked over or refused to pick up. After picking them up each time, Ms. Springfield dumped them out again and had Kyle pick them up. After doing this several times, she asked him, "Have you practiced cleaning up the blocks or do you need to continue?" In most cases, Kyle was happy to stop. On those days when Kyle threw a small tantrum and refused to clean up, Ms. Springfield used the hand-over-hand technique with him to assist him at cleaning up.

Recently Kyle had a severe temper tantrum in which he threw himself on the floor and kicked and screamed for several minutes. Knowing that the quiet chair would not be useful, Ms. Springfield placed him in time-out in the corner of the room. As she assisted him, practically carrying him, to the corner, she repeated, "Once you stop kicking and screaming and can get yourself together, you can return to join the class." After Kyle continued to throw a tantrum in the corner of the room, the teacher lost her patience and said firmly, "You calm down right now or I'll ship you out of this class." Upon hearing this, Kyle wailed louder and began kicking over chairs and other objects that were in his way. As his behavior escalated, the other children became clearly disturbed and frightened. A couple began to cry. This further intensified the environment. Finally, in an attempt to get Kyle to calm down, Ms. Springfield went to the corner and held Kyle down with her hands. Kyle eventually calmed down as he became tired. He was then taken to the office to see Ms. Dodd, who immediately called his father.

In each of four recent meetings with Kyle's father, Ms. Dodd has clearly explained Kyle's misbehavior while emphasizing her concern with his depressed, angry mood. Kyle has been a student at Rhodes for over a year. Although he has had some difficulties with temper tantrums in the past, his teachers have generally viewed him as a happy child on most days. Over the course of the month of October, his mood had shifted noticeably. Ms. Dodd explained to Kyle's father that the boy seemed preoccupied, worried, and sullen. He withdrew from socializing with the other children and fought with others, including his two best friends. Twice Ms. Springfield found him crying quietly in a corner by himself while the other children were playing.

While Ms. Springfield took Edna back to class, Ms. Dodd called Kyle's father at his office and requested that he come to Rhodes to meet with her. In the meantime, Mr. Desco had walked Kyle up to the director's office. The boy plopped himself firmly in a chair and started humming to himself. When Ms. Dodd asked him to tell what had happened in the classroom with Edna, he abruptly turned around in the seat and hid his head. He continued to hum to himself, but this time his humming turned angry. Ms. Dodd allowed him to sit and hum for a few minutes before interrupting him. Then she asked again, "Kyle, I want you to tell me about what happened in the classroom."

"Edna did it," Kyle blurted out.

"Edna did what?" Ms. Dodd asked. By now she was crouched on one knee in front of the lad, but Kyle refused to talk. He kept his head buried in the back of the seat and hummed to himself. Realizing she was going to get nowhere with Kyle, Ms. Dodd escorted him out to the secretary's office and seated him a large orange beanbag chair. "I have no choice but to get your dad in here to discuss this problem," Ms. Dodd remarked as she picked up the phone and called Kyle's dad at work.

Kyle's father, Mr. Ehlenbeck, is a very proud man who generally keeps his feelings close to his vest. He works as an engineer at a large defense industry corporation. When he arrived to meet with Ms. Dodd, the director explained the nature of the incident and once again voiced her concerns about Kyle's behavior and angry mood. Mr. Ehlenbeck said that he had seen no problems with Kyle at home. "Sure, he's going through a bit of a tough time with Sally and me being separated, but he'll be okay." When Ms. Dodd inquired further about the "tough time," Mr. Ehlenbeck became silent. He looked up at the ceiling for a second, gathered himself, and then spoke. "Kyle does fine when he's with me, but when he's with his mother—" Mr. Ehlenbeck halted abruptly as his voice began to creak with emotion.

"What days does Kyle spend with you?" Ms. Dodd asked.

"It varies from week to week. Sally and I each take him 2 days at a time," replied Kyle's father in a flat tone.

Ms. Dodd wrinkled her forehead quizzically. "Two days here, 2 days there? That's an unusual arrangement, Mr. Ehlenbeck. Most parents who are divorced—"

"We're only separated," Mr. Ehlenbeck corrected.

Ms. Dodd continued, "Most parents who are separated arrange for the child to stay with one parent during the week and one on the weekends. Switching back and forth every 2 days can be difficult on a 4-year-old child."

"Kyle's got no problem with it. The testing shows he's functioning intellectually more like a 5- or 6-year-old," Mr. Ehlenbeck countered. "He's a very grown-up little kid. And he gets to be with both of us equally. That's what important. If we did it the other way, Kyle would probably only see me on weekends. That's only 2 days out of 7, under 29% of the total time. Kyle needs more time than that with his father."

"That may be true, Mr. Ehlenbeck, but what concerns me is that Kyle may feel like he is always moving, never settling in long enough to feel at home."

Mr. Ehlenbeck became defensive. "You're talking as if this is a problem at home. Kyle's behavior is fine at both my place and with his mother. He only has behavior problems here. What does that tell you?"

"Well, I think we're doing the best we can with Kyle here, Mr. Ehlenbeck. I'm just concerned that—"

Mr. Ehlenbeck interrupted, "Aren't your teachers trained to work with preschool kids? This is supposed to be one of the best Montessoris in the county and you're telling me you can't handle a 4-year-old boy?"

Ms. Dodd paused for a moment. She could feel her temper rising. She wanted to defend her teachers and her program. She wanted to tell Kyle's father that he was wrong. She wanted to tell him that he and his wife needed to seek counseling for Kyle and themselves. But she also knew that she was walking a fine line. She knew that she had a very incomplete understanding of what was going on in the Ehlenbeck family. The classrooms at Rhodes, including Ms. Springfield's, were always looking to improve. She didn't want to simply throw all the blame on the parents and claim her school had no weaknesses. Her mind racing, she looked at Mr. Ehlenbeck and thought about what to say next. "Look," she began, "we have to develop a consistent program to get him back on track."

"Yeah, but Kyle does fine at home, nothin' a good swat won't fix," Mr. Ehlenbeck replied. Mrs. Dodd bit her tongue. She wanted to tell him that you can't just hit a child every time he gets out of line, that corporal punishment only encourages further violent behavior. Ms. Dodd stared an angry hole into Mr. Ehlenbeck's forehead. Mr. Ehlenbeck sighed and said that he had to get back to work. As he pulled himself out of the chair, Mr. Ehlenbeck remarked that maybe it was time to move Kyle to another school. Ms. Dodd shook her head and watched him walk away.

CASE **30**

THE WICKMAN MEMOIRS

 THE INCIDENT

When Seth first met Mr. Wickman, his fifth-grade science and social studies teacher, the aged and blunt-speaking veteran told the boy that he had better "work his butt off" this year if he hoped to pass. It was soon after these comments that Seth began to experience problems in Mr. Wickman's class. In his first day of the year speech, Bill Wickman would try to intimidate students in an attempt to show who was boss for the rest of the year. He would tell them that no one gets a break. He would say, "If you think you're a BMOC [Big Man on Campus] because you're some sports star, forget it. You will not get a break. You will have to work hard just like everyone else." He would frequently tease and taunt these same sports stars for the mistakes they made on the field. Seth too was a target on the first day. "Many of you think you're *special* with a capital *S*—well, don't expect a thing from me. Ya hear me, Seth Hanson—don't expect any breaks from me," Mr. Wickman shouted as he paced the aisles while trumpeting his first-day speech. Seth was slightly taken aback by his comments, as well as intimidated by the manner in which they were delivered to him. Mr. Wickman believed that if he established the upper hand in the classroom on day 1, then he would deal with few or no behavior problems all year.

Seth's second day was worse than the first. At the start of class, Mr. Wickman asked Seth to read a section of the textbook aloud. Seth was a weak oral reader whose skills tended to deteriorate markedly under duress. Mr. Wickman knew this, but his "everyone is treated equal" policy justified his right to have students fo whatever he wanted. As Seth stumbled over the words he read, he noticed Mr. Wickman becoming increasingly frustrated. Seth noticed that the other students were watching Mr. Wickman's facial expressions. When Seth stopped reading and looked up from his text, he saw Mr. Wickman grimacing and shaking his head as if he were agonized by Seth's reading difficulties. Before Seth could finish reading, Mr. Wickman cut him off in midsentence and remarked in an exasperated tone "Okay, okay, someone else needs to read." Unaccustomed to being treated in such a degrading manner, Seth broke into tears and ran out of class, a terribly embarrassing scene to an adolescent boy. Mr. Wickman let him go and told him, "Keep running all the way down to the principal's office for a detention slip."

The next day, during the science lesson, Seth decided to fight back by making goofy faces at his teacher, wildly exaggerating Mr. Wickman's facial expressions and body movements every time the man turned his back to write on the board. As the other students giggled, Mr. Wickman's anger grew. Each time he turned to write on the board, Seth imitated him. Unable to catch Seth in the act, Mr. Wickman finally held up class until someone confessed that Seth was the guilty party. In an explosive moment, Mr. Wickman grabbed Seth by the collar and physically assisted him down to the principal's office.

On other days, Seth passed notes calling him "Wickman the Weird Worm," referring to Mr. Wickman's shaved head and rather long neck. Seth was sneaky enough to get away with this mocking behavior on many days. When he did get caught, he was sent to the office for in-school-suspension (ISS). As Seth's "class clown" reputation grew among the other students, he began to imitate teachers in his other classes. Within two weeks of the initial incident, Mr. Wickman was sending Seth to the office on an almost daily basis for ISS.

BACKGROUND INFORMATION

Seth Hanson was first identified as having a learning disability (LD) and Attention Deficit Hyperactivity Disorder (ADHD) late in the year in fourth grade. Ms. Jones, his fourth-grade teacher, noticed problems early on and tried to help Seth. In particular, she noticed that Seth had reading problems and was easily distracted by noises and motion. Although he excelled in math (and loved it), he displayed weak reading comprehension skills and had difficulty maintaining attention to academic tasks for long periods of time. After Anne Jones completed some informal testing and the assessment specialist completed a battery of formal tests, it was determined that Seth met the criteria to receive learning disability services in the areas of reading and written language. At roughly the same time, he was diagnosed by a physician as having ADHD.

At his eligibility meeting, it was determined that because Seth needed assistance, he would spend the majority of his day in the general education setting, and he would receive itinerant, pull-out services from Kathy Spears, the LD teacher at the school. Mr. "Mack" Overton, his fifth-grade homeroom teacher, was also at the meeting. Mr. Overton worked closely with Kathy Spears and Anne Jones. Because the fourth- and fifth-grade teachers at the school each taught different disciplinary areas, they often worked closely together, like Mr. Overton and Ms. Jones. In Seth's case, these two teachers were constantly meeting to discuss his transition into fifth grade. Both cared deeply about each of their students and both were great teachers. Kathy Spears, on the other hand, was often so spread out across the school that she tended not to work closely with any other teachers.

Ms. Spears was a provisionally certified special education teacher and was only in her second year. Because of her limited training and massive caseload, she often struggled to meet the needs of her students. Kathy's inexperience and large caseload often resulted in students not getting sufficient services or receiving only cursory services from her. Kathy often felt that she was only doing educational triage, doing the best she could at any moment for those students who seemed to have the most urgent needs. Therefore, students with more severe or persistent learning problems received most of her time. Kathy worked full time during the day and went to college classes in the evening to complete her certification requirements. With only one year left on her provisional certification, she had to complete 15 credits over the upcoming year or lose her certification from the state Department of Education.

When Kathy first met Seth, she quickly noticed how smart he was and came to the conclusion that he probably wouldn't require many services or accommodations. Kathy decided to pull Seth out of his art class to receive reading instruction in the small space allotted to her, found behind the school's stage. The school was overcrowded and had very limited space. For Kathy, the small, secluded area behind the stage often served as her classroom. Except for lunches and play rehearsals, it was a relatively quiet area. On those days when it too noisy to teach, Kathy would carry her boxes of instructional materials and move her students to the library to work. She often asked her college advisor, Professor Kaplan, if it was legal for the school not to have a classroom available to educate the children on her caseload. His reply was that it was wrong, but there was little either of them could do about it. If she complained too loudly to the principal, she might be transferred to another school or worse. Seth would have to settle for the limited services that Kathy could provide.

When Kathy worked with Seth, they spent most of their time learning vocabulary and developing word attack skills. She never really sat down with Seth to explore which areas of reading he was having difficulty with, but assumed these were the primary ones based on his test results found in his psychological evaluation. Kathy had not spoken much with his teachers, Ms. Jones or Mr. Overton, about Seth's specific reading problems because of the mildness of Seth's disability and the large number of other students on her caseload. As she worked with him, she saw an improvement in his knowledge of vocabulary words (because of Seth's excellent memory) but not much improvement in his decoding skills. She claimed, "He just doesn't get it."

When the possibility of a learning disability diagnosis was first presented to Seth's parents, they were very reluctant to have him labeled. His father thought that he was just a precocious boy and feared that the label would brand him for life. As for his ADHD, medication was not an option. As far as the parents were concerned, drugs were not the solution to their son's problems. His parents began getting Seth involved in sports with the hope that he would channel his excessive energy and improve his concentration. In regard to Seth's difficulties in getting along with his peers, a struggle that had become obvious in a series of fights at the bus stop and on the playground, they felt that Seth's tendency to be aggressive and forceful was typical for an active boy. "Boys will be boys," was a statement frequently spoken by his mother. His father too pointed out that he himself never really did well at reading, yet he ended up becoming a successful corporate accountant.

Anne Jones and Mack Overton thought that it was strange that Seth had made it so far without being identified as LD because, as they looked over his records, they saw many of the telltale signs of a student with a serious learning problem. As his records revealed, Seth earned many grades of C and D in reading and other content areas, and many of his past teachers wrote comments that he was "inattentive," "immature," and "impulsive" in class. Despite these signs, they also knew that past teachers were reluctant to recommend borderline students for formal evaluation because of the extensive paperwork and tracking forms that had to be filed. Also, in many cases, classroom teachers believed that they were the best person to attempt to help Seth. Anne also knew that because of the small class sizes in the school, his past teachers probably were able to give Seth much individual attention. In fact, even after being identified as LD by the school, Seth was able to receive almost all of his support services in his general education classes.

Through a combination of his own compensatory strategies and instructional adaptations from past teachers, for the most part Seth was able to pass his classes. For example, Seth developed good listening comprehension skills. By the time he entered Mr. Overton's class, he learned to master the art of listening comprehension; that is, he was able to listen to others, repeat their words to himself, and, for the most part, understand and remember. In addition, in most of Seth's elementary school classes, the teacher would have the class take turns reading the textbook aloud, yet another advantage for Seth. He could listen to passages that he would have trouble reading. Moreover, when Seth went home in the evening, his mother or father would help him with his homework. Despite the long hours working on his homework, Seth was very diligent and always completed each assignment. On a number of occasions, Seth would get up early in the morning to finish any homework assignments that he couldn't complete the night before.

Anne and Mack met frequently to discuss Seth's problems and progress over lunch in the teacher's lounge. Soon they began to hear that Seth was exhibiting similar disruptive behaviors in other classes. In Trudy Miller's literature class, Seth had begun talking excessively to other students. As a result of his excessive talking, he often missed information in his notes. When he went to study, his incomplete notes prevented him from preparing well for tests and, consequently, he began failing many tests and quizzes. It wasn't long before his teachers began to discuss moving Seth to a more restrictive environment, meaning a full-time learning disabilities classroom. For Seth this meant moving to a new school. It was something that no one wanted, but with his problems accumulating, there seemed to be limited options available. Many felt that soon they would have to hold another meeting to discuss Seth's behavior and his options.

Seth's parents, Stanley and Judy Hanson, loved his teachers—Anne and Mack. To them, Ms. Jones was a loving, caring teacher who was always willing to spend extra time working with Seth. Likewise, Mr. Overton was a great mentor and tutor for Seth. For both Anne and Mack, the relationship was reciprocal. They knew that Seth would always come to school with completed assignments and they knew that Seth's parents would always support any educational decision concerning Seth's future. Through after-school meetings and Saturday morning brunches, the Hansons and Mack and Anne all became close friends. When Seth's troubles erupted in fifth grade, it was Anne who made the phone call on the first day of school to Seth's parents.

As Judy Hanson explained to Anne, Seth had the misfortune of being placed in Mr. Wickman's class. Anne had warned the Hansons about Mr. Wickman, but she tended to sugarcoat her negative description of him so as not to cause the Hansons any unnecessary worry. Plus, she hesitated to speak negatively about a faculty colleague. As Judy spoke to Anne, she asked about his reputation. Anne replied that Bill Wickman had been in the school system for a number of years and was considered a "tough" teacher. When Judy pressed Anne for more details, she finally admitted that Mr. Wickman had taught fifth grade for 20 years and had earned the reputation of being a cantankerous, burned-out instructor who no longer enjoyed teaching and was disliked by most of his students. The school's principal repeatedly "encouraged" Mr. Wickman to retire, but the teacher stayed on because he was tenured and was only a few years away from a retirement with full benefits.

Instead of learning science or social studies, Mr. Wickman's students often sat through long drawn-out stories about his recent divorce, the foibles of dating, and his impending retirement to the coast of Texas. Mr. Wickman was from an "old school of thought" that believed that students with disabilities were either "stupid" or "lazy." On more than one occasion he was overheard saying about students with LD that, "It's all in their heads. We cater too much to these kids. All they really need is tougher standards and strict teachers." After 30 minutes of this conversation, Anne finally managed to calm down Judy and advise her to give Seth a chance to adjust to his difficult new environment. All kids have to learn to deal with an occasional difficult teacher. Seth deserved a chance.

Two weeks later, as Anne was walking into her house, the phone rang. Again, it was Judy reporting that Mr. Wickman had made some harsh comments to Seth about "being lazy" and "getting an attitude adjustment." Anne was surprised to hear the comments, but not shocked; she had heard similar from other students, but felt that students were exaggerating his words.

"Look, Judy, maybe you had better set up an appointment with the principal, Mr. Pearson, and Mr. Wickman to discuss his comments," Anne urged. Judy agreed and a meeting was set for Friday. As Friday approached, Seth began to complain about Mr. Wickman sneering at him in class and again making fun of him. Seth claimed that Mr. Wickman compared him to a delicate little bird that was afraid to leave its nest.

As Judy walked into the office that Friday, her anger had reached its pinnacle. When she shook Mr. Pearson's hand, she remarked, "Mr. Pearson, if my son's reports are true, this guy Wickman is a jerk." From the corner of the room Mr. Wickman sneered and remarked, "Nice to meet you too. Oh, by the way, your son doesn't know what he's talking about." After sitting down, Judy began to hear a barrage of complaints about Seth from Mr. Wickman. Arriving late, Kathy Spears remarked that she had not heard anything about Seth having behavior or attitude problems, and from what she knew, he was a good student.

CASE **31**

FRUSTRATED BY MATH

THE INCIDENT

Robert Simone plopped down at his desk with a loud bang and began murmuring to himself how much he hated school. When he saw the worksheet that had been placed on his desk by his teacher, Mr. Doyle, Robert began shaking his head back and forth. As part of Mr. Doyle's daily routine, he often left assignments on each student's desk for them to work on as soon as they arrived in class. Mr. Doyle did not believe in down time and ensured smooth transitions by having students immediately move from one task to the next. As the rest of the students filed in to his class, Mr. Doyle sat quietly at his own desk grading papers. As students piled their coats in their cubbies and took their seats, Mr. Doyle finished grading one more paper.

Within minutes of sitting down, Robert began muttering again to himself, "I don't wanna do this. I don't wanna do this." When Mr. Doyle looked up from his desk, Robert had already let out a loud yell and banged his head down on the desk. Robert was supposed to be completing a worksheet of 20 addition problems. After completing only five of the problems, he gave up because he felt they were too difficult. Instead of working on math, he was now scribbling cartoon skulls on his paper. Robert had avoid completing assignments in the past by using similar stalling techniques. He often had problems completing difficult or frustrating tasks, particularly in the afternoon. So persistent was this problem that his IEP included an objective on increasing Robert's ability to complete assigned tasks. In the morning, he typically completed all of his assignments, but by the afternoon Robert was often sleepy and inattentive and thus found it more difficult to complete assignments.

After Robert's outburst, Mr. Doyle went to Robert's desk and tried to redirect him back to his worksheet. "Now, come on, Robert. You can answer these problems," he said as pointed to the worksheet. "We did the same kind yesterday and you were able to do them," Mr. Doyle encouraged Robert.

"These things are too hard," complained Robert. Following this comment, he let out a loud yell, "I don't wanna work on this and you can't make me." With that, the other students let out a simultaneous "Ooohhh." They had witnessed similar confrontations before in class and they to knew that the end result would be Robert spending part of his day in time-out. With the attention of other students now focused on him, Robert slyly let a grin slip over his face.

Mr. Doyle, who was now becoming visibly agitated, said, "Look, get to work or you get to go to the corner." "The corner" was Mr. Doyle's version of time-out. Despite his teacher's threat, Robert sat in his seat motionless, overcome with stubbornness. Noticing all the small eyes watching him, Mr. Doyle felt that he was losing control of the situation and his class. As Robert contemplated his limited options, Mr. Doyle snapped at the other students, "Get back to work." Quickly their heads went down as they got back to their worksheets. Next, he looked at Robert and said firmly, "*Get to work.*" The other students knew that Mr. Doyle meant business and suddenly the classroom became quiet. Again, he waited several seconds to see what Robert was going to do and when he saw no movement from Robert, he directed him again to get to work. Robert did not budge.

"That's it! You lose recess!" Mr. Doyle said as he marched to the board. In bold letters he wrote on the board, "ROBERT." By now Mr. Doyle was seething with anger at what he perceived to be a lost battle. With the chalk cracking, he finished writing "NO RECESS." Realizing the seriousness of Robert's offense, a few other students chimed in, "You're in trouble now, Robbie." To this, Robert defiantly held up the worksheet in the air and ripped it in half. What followed next was a loss of two tokens and a trip to time-out. Once in time-out, Robert began loud wailing and crying, occasionally blurting out that Mr. Doyle was unfair and that he hated him.

The day after this incident, Mr. Doyle decided to discuss Robert's behavior with his classroom aide, Kelly Stellar. Ms. Stellar told him that Robert got into a heated discussion with another student on the playground immediately before coming to math class. In her description of the playground incident, it was Jacob, a rather intimidating boy from another class, who sparked the quarrel.

In Ms. Stellar's words, "Robert was playing nicely with another student when he was suddenly hit with a red playground ball. As Robert picked up the ball, Jacob started lashing out at Robert, insulting him and telling him that he was interfering in the game. When Jacob went back to his game, Robert appeared to calm down. But, when I asked him to line up, he angrily mumbled something and slowly walked over to the line. Once inside, as we were walking down the hall, I could tell that he was upset about something. He wouldn't talk to me. He just threw his coat angrily into the closet and stormed off to his desk."

BACKGROUND INFORMATION

Robert is an 11-year-old categorized as having a mild developmental disability who currently attends Tannerville Elementary School in downtown Gatesburg. Robert is tall for his age, the tallest student in class. The fact that he towers over most other students may be part of the reason why he has a reputation for bullying other students. The other students often keep a fair distance between them and Robert during games and other activities. Robert has been in Mr. Doyle's self-contained special education class for 2 years and has had conflicts with Mr. Doyle on a number of other occasions.

Robert scored 68 on the Wechsler Intelligence Scale for Children. Robert's academic skills in all of the basic skill areas, reading, math, and written language, are commensurate with that IQ score, roughly on the second-grade level. Robert has also been identified as having Attention Deficit Hyperactivity Disorder (ADHD) and currently takes Ritalin to help control his attention and hyperactivity. Mr. Doyle often complains that Robert has either outgrown his prescribed dosage of Ritalin or has become immune to its effects.

Robert lives with his mother, Daphne, in a nearby apartment. Robert is the only child and Ms. Simone, a single mom, works during the day and relies on Robert to get home from his bus stop by himself. He usually plays video games or watches TV for about an hour before his mother arrives home. Then she immediately gets him working on his homework and completing his chores.

Ms. Simone is very concerned with Robert's slow progress in school. Mr. Doyle has often told her that he wishes his other students' parents were as involved in their child's education as she is in Robert's. Ms. Simone is familiar with Robert's stubbornness and behavioral problems. At home, Robert frequently refuses to complete work for her and often runs away from home for short periods of time when confronted with a distressing problem. Ms. Simone has relayed to Mr. Doyle that morning is the time of day when these problem generally occur. During the morning hours, Ms. Simone often has great difficulty waking Robert and getting him ready for school. Even though he goes to bed early enough each night, he is very sluggish and resistant in the morning. He does not like to go to school. He would rather sleep or watch TV all day. She knows her son well, so it came as no surprise when she received a note that night from Mr. Doyle describing the incident during math. When she spoke to Robert about the incident, he refused to discuss it.

Ms. Simone has difficulty dealing with Robert and often punishes him by taking away privileges like TV or Xbox video games. When Robert was younger (and smaller), she would spank him when he wouldn't listen to her or when he talked back to her. Now that he is older, she is hesitant to physically discipline him because she is afraid that he will strike her back. She is also afraid of unintentionally encouraging him to use force and violence in his interactions with students at school. In the past, she asked Mr. Doyle for suggestions as to how she could better manage Robert's behavior at home. Mr. Doyle recommended that Robert lose privileges and that she try time-out at home by restricting him to his room. She too has had mixed results with Robert. During many confrontations, she ends up on the losing end of the battle. Even when she "wins," she doesn't feel satisfied that Robert is really learning how to behave in more cooperative and positive ways.

In a recent problem behavior incident, Robert stole candy from a store, Willie's Stop & Go. Robert stopped off at this corner convenience store on his way home from school. He was caught by the store clerk stuffing a bag of candy in his pocket. Fortunately for Robert, the store clerk called his mother and not the police. Ms. Simone came from work as soon as heard what had happened. She apologized, paid the clerk, made Robert apologize, and rushed him home for his punishment. Once at home, she reprimanded him and questioned him numerous times as to why he stole the candy. Robert responded that he was hungry, had no money, and didn't think they would notice if one bag of candy was missing. Ms. Simone decided that Robert's punishment would be to lose the use of his video games and TV for 2 weeks. Upon hearing this, Robert stormed out of the house shouting, "It's not fair!" and "My mom is a mean witch!" Despite her commands for him to return, Robert was gone. Within an hour, Robert returned home and went silently to his room. It was a long 2 weeks for both Robert and Ms. Simone.

Mr. Doyle frequently finds himself pondering how he handles Robert's unusual behavior. After one tough day, he began to ask himself a series of questions: "Did I handle it properly? Could I have not gotten so angry? Should I have immediately put him in the corner?" Only in his second year of teaching, Mr. Doyle still isn't quite certain how to handle many of his students' problems. He remembers back to his college class in behavior management, but draws a blank as to what he could have done differently. An admitted "control freak" at heart, Mr. Doyle likes a quiet, orderly, business-like classroom. In the past, he has been able to manage many of his students' diffcult and challenging behaviors, but Robert's behavior has consistently become worse as the school year has progressed.

Mr. Doyle tries to make his class a rewarding and positive experience for his students. His classroom management system consists of the use of a token economy and time-out. This technique has worked well on some days, but it has been horrible on others. He rewards students with tokens after every class period (about every 50 minutes). He awards them one token for completing an assignment and one token for appropriate behavior during that time period. Despite the rewards, students are often off-task and out of their seats. Mr. Doyle uses the threat of losing tokens as one way to maintain his students' attention to tasks and to redirect them back to work.

Robert has both successful and less successful days earning tokens. On those less successful days, Robert did not earn tokens because he was talking, wandering around out of his seat, disrupting other students, making noises or tapping his foot or pencil, and complaining about his work. Most of these same behaviors also prevented him from completing his work. In addition to these behaviors, every few days Robert would become so upset at his lack of tokens that he would throw the few he had in the trash. Of course, having only a few or no tokens prevented him from earning the prizes at the token exchange that occurred every Friday afternoon.

Both Ms. Simone and Mr. Doyle recognize that Robert has behavior problems that are usually exasperated by his inability to control his anger. It seems that often Robert only makes bad situations worse by getting angry and losing control of his behavior (i.e., swearing, hitting, etc.). In class, when Robert's behavior escalated because of his anger, Mr. Doyle would try to calm him down by placing him in timeout. In many cases, Robert would eventually calm down after about 15 minutes and he would be able to return to class. Once Robert was back in class, Mr. Doyle would require him to complete the assignment that he was working on prior to the incident. Despite his limited success with calming Robert down, Mr. Doyle was hesitant to try other anger control techniques with Robert because he felt that he would be reinforcing Robert's inappropriate behavior. In many ways, Mr. Doyle was a behaviorist at heart.

As the only special education teacher in the school, Mr. Doyle feels that he has to "walk on eggshells" around the other teachers and the principal. The principal, Ms. Gunnison, has a no-nonsense type of management style. She is the type of administrator that would rather suspend a student than seriously discuss the reasons for a student's inappropriate behavior. Mr. Doyle was chosen as the very first special education teacher at Tannerville Elementary School because of his diplomatic style while conferring with other teachers. He was told by his special education supervisor that he needs to establish a good working relationship with the other faculty so that next year they can try to place other special education classes in the school. Despite the inroads he was making with other faculty, he often felt restrained because he had to handle all of the behavior problems in his classroom, instead of allowing the principal to handle some of the incidents.

CASE **32**

PULLED AT THE EDGES

THE INCIDENT

Eric was seated in the last row of the large bus. The eight other students in his class were scattered across the many rows of seats. Nicholas and Edgar were pinching each other on the neck and giggling. Laura and Kip were as quiet as ever, her eyes seemingly gazing out the window. Mahoney rocked back and forth, humming and hugging her hands to her chest like a football. Mr. Edwards and Ms. Stevens were seated together at the center of the bus, some eight rows in front of Eric. As usual, they were planning the day's events at the last minute, fleshing out the details on the bus ride on the way to the activity. This was Ms. Stevens's style, all planning at the last moment, and she was very comfortable with this approach. Mr. Edwards was annoyed with her for putting them in the "hurry-up planning" mode one more time.

Eric looked down at the box of bag lunches resting on the seat in front of him. He suddenly realized that there would be no hot lunch served in the cafeteria today, that bag lunches consisting of sandwiches had been packed instead. He started crying, at first very softly, and then gradually louder and fuller. By the time the small yellow bus carrying Ms. Stevens's class was driving down Interstate 95 Eric's tears had escalated up to a full howl.

"Oh, I should have seen this one coming," groaned Mr. Edwards, the classroom aide. He jumped quickly back to sit next to Eric.

Ms. Stevens smiled and shrugged her shoulders. "Par for the course," she said with an attitude of acceptance.

Mr. Edwards turned to Eric. "Come on, Eric, you ate the bologna sandwich last week. Remember? I put the spicy mustard on it for you." Mr. Edwards tried to calm Eric down. Noticing that Eric seemed to take some pleasure in remembering the mustard, Mr. Edwards repeated the phrase "spreading the mustard" while pretending to spread mustard along the top of Eric's hand. This gradually soothed Eric and turned into a friendly little game with Mr. Edwards rubbing Eric's hand.

While Mr. Edwards helped Eric settle down, Irving started shouting and bouncing in his seat. He kept pointing at Sara. Sara was seated two rows in front of Eric, and Irving was sitting in his wheelchair directly behind Sara. Sara's face was

149

tucked tightly between the seatback and the window, hidden from the adults' view. Irving hadn't noticed anything wrong until he saw blood on the window. The blood reminded him of a scary movie he had once watched about a very bad man in a hockey mask. He screamed.

The bus pulled up to the curb in front of the Overland Mall. Ms. Stevens rushed over to find out what Irving was upset about. Sara was bleeding from a broken scab at the edge of her mouth. She had pressed her face against the window and smeared a streak of blood on the window pane. As she pulled at the corner of her mouth with an index finger, the cut widened and more blood rolled down the side of her face. The other students, all middle schoolers categorized as having moderate to severe levels of developmental disabilities, were becoming increasingly distressed by the commotion.

BACKGROUND INFORMATION

Sara is a 13-year-old girl with cerebral palsy. School records describe her as functioning intellectually within the severe range of intellectual disability. Teachers and parents who know her well describe her as having a wide range of skills—sometimes called *splinter skills*—that diverge sharply from the "severe mental retardation" diagnosis. For instance, often Sara seems to be very intuitive in her relationships with others, connected in an emotional and empathic way to close friends and family. If someone she cares about is upset or in pain, Sara often notices and responds quickly to the person's emotional distress. She is very kind and supportive to her classmates.

In the past 6 months, Sara's teachers have noticed her exhibiting some autistic or autistic-like behaviors. She does not speak in words, although she understands a variety of words and sentences spoken to her. At times, she isolates herself and does not notice people and events in her immediate environment. She has engaged in behaviors that the staff calls "self-stimulatory," mainly poking and squeezing her cheeks with her fingers. The mildest form of this involves repetitive tapping on the hollows of her cheeks. In the most severe form of this behavior, Sara places her fingers under her lips at the corner of her mouth and yanks outward repeatedly. Over time, this has caused the corners of her mouth to become red, inflamed, and split wide open. At the time of this incident, the edges of Sara's mouth were encrusted with large scabs.

Concerned with the recent frequency and severity of Sara's self-injurious behavior, Ms. Stevens and Mr. Edwards conducted a brief functional analysis. For 3 weeks, they observed Sara very closely. For each of the instances when she tugged on her lip with her fingers, they wrote down the contextual factors present immediately before, during, and after the behavior. These factors included environmental conditions such as physical space and materials, learning activities, interactions with peers or adults, and interactions with stimulating or interesting objects. The purpose of this analysis was to try to figure out what specific environmental conditions seemed to support or even provoke Sara's behavior.

They found that the mouth-tugging behavior occurred in some form or another once in week 1, twice in week 2, and four times in the third week. Of the seven instances, six took place during the final hour of school. The single other occurrence was in the morning just before lunch. They found no pattern in relation to her interactions with peers or in regard to the kinds of learning activities that Sara was working on at the time of the behavior.

Based on six instances in the final hour of school, Ms. Stevens has concluded that Sara becomes worn out late in the day, and that this exhaustion (and perhaps also boredom) contributes to this behavior. Her opinion is backed up by the fact that Sara often puts her head down on her desk in the afternoon, ostensibly because she is becoming tired.

Mr. Edwards disagrees. He says that Sara puts her head on her desk at all times of day. He admits that she often does this more in the afternoon, but he says that she isn't tired. She likes the feeling of the cool, smooth desktop against her cheek. Sometimes she rubs her face back and forth slowly as if to soothe herself.

Based on the functional analysis data, Ms. Stevens and Mr. Edwards found that Sara tended to grab her lip when she became upset or anxious. This anxiety could be triggered by many kinds of stimuli, many different kinds of activities or events taking place around her, but often (five instances out of seven) the behavior immediately followed episodes of loud and dramatic behavior by Eric. Sara and Eric had been classmates in special programs together since the first day each entered public school. Though they rarely played together, Sara seemed to be particularly tuned in to Eric's emotions and behavior. When he was upset or agitated, Sara was likely to follow.

Based on this knowledge, Sara's teachers tried two specific strategies to reduce Sara's self-injurious behavior. First, they often organized learning activities in such a way as to keep Sara and Eric physically separated. Eric would be seated on one side of the room and Sara on the other. That way, if Eric became upset, Sara might not even know. His influence would be diminished by distance. The second strategy involved analyzing and addressing the kinds of situations and conditions that tended to upset Eric. The teachers reasoned that if they could learn to keep Eric settled down, that calm would help Sara, too. They started to collect data describing the context—when, where, the activity, as many details as possible—whenever Eric became very upset. They also decided to interview Eric's parents and his older sister, Terry, a student at a local college who always has strong insight into Eric's emotions and reactions. These interviews might provide them with more understanding about why Eric felt upset during the school day. The incident on the school bus detailed here occurred on the third day of the implementation of these new strategies. The interviews with Eric's family members are scheduled for the following week.

During the past two years, Sara has lived at the Weldon Home, a small foster care facility for children with intellectual disabilities. The decision to place her at Weldon was very difficult for her parents and sister. They held a strong belief that Sara belonged at home with her family. But her behavior had deteriorated. She sometimes flew into wild tantrums, breaking toys and furniture, sometimes injuring herself in the process. She was growing too large for her mother, father, grandmother, and sister to physically control. Because of Sara's increasingly difficult behavior at home, the family had little choice but to seek outside support. They were saddened to find that hiring qualified caregivers to assist in their home was beyond their financial means and beyond the policies of the county agency in charge of residential support programs.

Disability service providers in many areas typically arranged to provide support staff within the client's home. The philosophy behind this practice was that people generally do better remaining in their own homes with their own families. Neither disability nor a need for assistance should be a rationale to break up families. Instead of moving the individual to the services (such as an institution or group home), the support would simply go directly to her in her home. But the local county disability agency still only paid for out-of-home placements for disabled persons with significant needs. They ran a series of group homes, and they provided no in-home support services. An out-of-home placement was the family's only alternative.

After an extensive search into local placement options, Sara's parents settled on the Weldon Home, a facility that houses eight teenaged girls with developmental disabilities and/or autism. The staff is knowledgeable and caring. Unfortunately, it is located 62 miles away from the family's home. This makes family visits during the week very difficult. Also, Sara had to change schools, shifting from the special school for students with severe disabilities that she had attended for many years to Ms. Steven's self-contained classroom at a middle school near the Weldon Home. Although the living arrangements at Weldon and the middle school class seemed good enough, Sara's family never felt fully comfortable with the decision to move her out of their home. They felt guilty and feared that they had somehow failed Sara by not somehow figuring out how to better support her within the family's home.

For many years her parents and her younger sister had enjoyed Sara's company in their home. The family enjoyed weekends at the lake with Sara's grandparents. As a young child, Sara always enjoyed riding in the family motorboat. She also had a special connection to her grandmother, a 73-year-old woman who plays Woody Guthrie songs on the guitar and has a complete collection of Fred Astaire musicals on DVD. There were some days when the entire family would go fishing and swimming, leaving young Sara curled up in her grandmother's arms and listening to stories: silly tales about railroad stations in the clouds, sailors who come home to their sweethearts, and woolly sheep that sing Irish ditties. When the family finally returned for dinner at the end of the day, they'd find Sara and her grandmother in that same spot on the wicker couch with an old army blanket tossed across them to hold off the evening chill.

Over the past year, Sara's grandmother has become ill. She is a diabetic, and her blood sugar level has become irregular. One more than one occasion, she has awoken in the early hours of morning with a queasy, weak feeling. Sara's grandfather would immediately give her some orange juice to bring her sugar up. Her diabetes is accompanied by hypertension and heart disease. Her doctors have struggled to find a group of medications to handle the various diseases without overwhelming side effects.

Due to her weakened condition, Sara's grandmother is often unable to make the trip to the Weldon Home to visit her granddaughter. Because Sara comes home almost every weekend, the two are able to spend some time together about once or twice each month. During these visits, Sara has thrown tantrums when she has not been allowed to curl up in her grandmother's lap. She doesn't understand (or doesn't accept) that she has grown too large and her grandmother has become too weak to hold her.

Sara's teacher is Ms. Stevens, a fifth-year special education teacher. She has dramatically changed the curriculum of this class to involve the students more in community activities. The tradition has been to keep students with severe mental disabilities sequestered in their classroom at the far southern wing of Callahan Middle School. Ms. Stevens has surprised her principal by talking her students into the community twice each week. Although her principal has expressed some ambivalence about "shaking things up unnecessarily," he also has arranged for bus transportation for these trips. In the past 2 weeks, however, he has received three phone calls from concerned parents of students in Ms. Stevens's class who claim that the trips into the community have somehow caused their children to have increased instances of misbehavior at home. These reports have been vague, and the connection between the community activities and the students' behavior struggles at home has been unclear to both the principal and Ms. Stevens. But the principal is concerned. He definitely does not like fielding phone calls from complaining parents. He would prefer not to have to deal with these parents, and he has communicated that concern to Ms. Stevens.

Mr. Edwards is an elderly gentleman who has been a special education classroom aide for 36 years. Ms. Stevens is the third teacher he has worked with in his 9 years in the self-contained class at Callahan Middle School. He considers himself to be the backbone of the program, the one constant bringing much-needed order to this classroom over the years. He has seen a number of educational fads come and go. There was a time when he had to hold a clipboard and count student behaviors all day. That was when the district was big on behavior modification. That faded, and activity-based teaching rolled in. Hands on. Hands on. Ms. Edwards grew tired of the students getting themselves and their hands into everything. It was easier when they didn't work in groups, when each student just stayed at his own desk. And now, with the positive behavior support training in the district, Mr. Edwards feared that he'd be stuck with a clipboard counting behaviors again.

Mr. Edwards is skeptical about Ms. Stevens's enthusiasm for bringing the students into to community. He would rather protect them from failure and the staring eyes of the public by remaining within the classroom. He has remained very wary about the whole "community integration" and "inclusion" movements. He doesn't believe that the mainstream world will ever accept his students the way they are. Additionally, Mr. Edwards claims that the community trips only reduce the structure and routine of the program, thereby increasing the negative behavior of the students.

Sara's class consists of students from 12 to 15 years old. There are six boys and three girls. Sara is one of four students in the class who do not speak. The other students vary in their expressive language skills. All the students have some degree of receptive language skills, although Mr. Edwards and Ms. Stevens frequently disagree about what the students understand or do not understand. In Mr. Edwards's opinion, the students understand almost everything that is going on around them. Sometimes, some of the students pretend not to understand what the adults are saying to them in order to get their way. Ms. Stevens tends to stick to what the speech and language specialist's reports say about each student's linguistic capabilities, even when she notices fairly obvious evidence that a student comprehends more than what the standardized tests say. In Sara's case, Mr. Edwards believes that she understands 80–90% of what is said to her or the conversations going on around her. The speech and language testing completed 8 months earlier indicate a far lower ability to comprehend spoken English.